Anger Management

The 21-Day Mental Makeover to Take Control of Your Emotions and Achieve Freedom from Anger, Stress, and Anxiety

PUBLISHED BY: James W. Williams

Copyright © 2019 All rights reserved.

Table of Contents

Your Free Gift

As a way of saying thanks for your purchase, I wanted to offer you a free bonus E-book called ***Bulletproof Confidence,*** exclusive to the readers of this book.

To get instant access, just go to:

https://theartofmastery.com/confidence/

Inside the book, you will discover:

- What are shyness and social anxiety, and the psychology behind them
- Simple yet powerful strategies for overcoming social anxiety
- Breakdown of the traits of what makes a confident person
- Traits you must DESTROY if you want to become confident
- Easy techniques you can implement TODAY to keep the conversation flowing
- Confidence checklist to ensure you're on the right path of self-development

PART 1

Anger – A Cry for Help or a Desire to Control?

Day 1

What is Anger?

Anger as a Powerful Emotion

Anger is a feeling we are all familiar with, although we experience it and express it in different ways. The usual cause of anger is a reaction to an unfair decision or treatment, as well as to criticism, being embarrassed in public, being bullied, feeling impatient, somebody's rude behavior, being ignored, losing, being dumped, and many more unpleasant experiences.

However, while anger is a perfectly natural part of life, it's not something we should encourage. On the contrary—most people try to control their anger, especially in social situations. Perhaps there were times in the distant past when being openly angry was a crucial survival skill, but in the sophisticated and densely-populated world we now live in, different survival techniques will help you succeed.

Like with so many other things in life, there are two sides to anger—it can be both a positive and a negative force in your life. On the upside, anger often serves as a sign that things are not right and that something needs to be done about the situation, like if you are facing unfair treatment, having to deal with rude people, or standing in a queue for too long. However, we often make ourselves angry by having unrealistic expectations.

The downside of anger, especially out-of-control anger, includes a long list of behaviors that lead to ruined relationships, domestic violence, imprisonment, destroyed health, spoiled opportunities, and more.

Often, the so-called primary anger masks the emotions that are the real reason for our aggression. The most common secondary emotions leading to anger are fear—often manifested as anxiety and worry—as well as sadness, because of a real or imaginary loss.

The reason these feelings cause anger is that fear and sadness make people feel vulnerable or threatened, and to stop themselves from becoming overwhelmed with these emotions, people often shift into anger mode. A friend of mine once said that it was only when she was behaving aggressively that she felt truly alive.

By shifting your fear of being dumped by your partner into anger, you subconsciously give yourself a shot of adrenalin, which makes you feel energized and in charge rather than helpless and vulnerable.

If used positively, this boost of energy can actually help you get out of a tricky situation or find a better resolution to a problem. However, if creating this false sense of confidence and control over the situation means you actually become aggressive and start abusing others, the adrenalin rush that created this powerful feeling will probably create more problems rather than offering any solutions.

Self-Anger

Turning your anger and frustration inward, whether you are aware of it or not, is one of the most self-destructive things you can do to yourself.

If you're angry with yourself for not being more attractive, more successful, or happily married, start by asking yourself what's stopping you from getting what you want. If you stay with this question for a while, you'll realize that you either don't really want these things or that the effort of getting them would outweigh any benefits you'd see.

Unfortunately, not having what you'd like or think you deserve is often the result of choices you made in the past which you are now paying for—wrong life partner, wrong investment decision, remaining in a dead-end job, and so on.

Not having what you want is a complicated issue, especially if the reason you can't get something is beyond your control, as things often are. Although having dreams can be a powerful motivating force that can help you overcome setbacks, having unrealistic dreams or not doing enough to make them happen will only make you sad, resentful, and—worst of all— angry at yourself for not having tried harder.

We usually turn anger outward, to other people—like the government, a particular person, or even life in general. However, those who turn their anger inward, toward themselves, usually reach a point where it manifests as self-hatred or rejection of certain aspects of self that they believe are a cause of their failure in life. So, like how in extreme situations, anger can lead to murder, self-anger can similarly lead to suicide.

Anger comes in many disguises—as resentment, ranting and raving, or blame. But it can also be masked by such feelings like impatience, envy, guilt, or low self-esteem.

So, what to do if you are openly or secretly angry at yourself? Besides learning anger management, you can do one of two things.

2 things to do when feeling angry at yourself:

- **Forgive yourself**

  Your failure to be what you think you should be or have what you think you deserve could be due to wrong life choices, or simply unrealistic expectations. However, while acknowledging your mistakes is necessary before you can move forward, beating yourself up over something you did or failed to do will get you nowhere. Instead of wallowing in your guilt or self-hatred, learn from your mistakes, face your demons (guilty thoughts, hurt feelings, disappointment) and stop replaying over and over again in your head that you're a failure. If you can forgive others, why can't you forgive yourself?

- **Work out why you're angry**

  If the reason for your anger is justified, do something about it. If it isn't, don't stress yourself by constantly thinking about how unfair life is, how ungrateful children can be, how selfish, rude, or arrogant people are.

If you think you deserve better and believe you can use your anger to make others aware of the injustice done to you, doing what you think may improve the situation.

However, don't forget that anger often breeds more anger, as well as resentment and fear. To prevent self-destructive behaviors and thoughts, stop thinking about the past (and your failures) and shift your focus to the present (and new opportunities).

Learn to Understand Your Anger

Before you try to control your anger, you have to make sure you understand what is causing it—what is REALLY causing it.

Next time you feel angry, try to calm down so you can think clearly about what's making you mad. This is not easy and you'll probably need to try more than once, because we often become masters at fooling ourselves.

4 steps in understanding your anger:

1. **Acknowledge your anger**

   Stop telling yourself (and others) "I'm fine." You can't be fine if deep down you are seething with rage.

Unless you acknowledge you have a problem, you won't be able to start looking for a solution.

2. Identify the key feeling behind your anger

This can be tricky, but if you are used to tuning into your emotions, it won't be too difficult. Emotional intelligence is a tool that can help you understand your emotions, and why your anger often masks more intense emotions such as disappointment, loneliness, or abandonment.

3. Ask yourself why

Once you work out what really fuels your anger, be brutally honest with yourself and admit why the fear, sadness, envy, or any other secondary emotion is making you so upset. For example, you may fear the future (if you believe you will be made redundant soon), you may fear loneliness (if you suspect your partner is contemplating leaving you), you may fear death (if you know you have a serious health issue), you may feel sad (because you let someone down), you may feel resentful (because of missed opportunities), you may feel envious (because amongst all your friends, you are the only one still living with your parents).

4. Deal with the secondary emotion

There are issues that can be resolved, and those that are beyond your control. If your anger stems from something that can be changed or improved, work on addressing this so you can close that chapter of your life and move on.

If your anger is caused by a secondary emotion, like fear, guilt, or anxiety, you should find a way to express this feeling in a healthy way.

When you understand what your anger is actually about, it will become much easier to find a way to deal with it. Although figuring out what is making you angry will not make the anger go away, it will at least help you keep it under control.

Anger is a very powerful emotion. The trick is to use its energy as fuel to motivate yourself to improve your life and get where you want to be.

Food for Thought:

1. Think of a time when you were very angry. Try to remember how you felt, how you looked, and how you behaved at the time. Do you think your reaction was justified? How would you react in the same situation today?

2. List three things that make you most angry. Why?

3. How do you react when you witness an angry outburst in public? Do you pretend not to see or hear anything? Do you try to get as far away as fast as you can? Or do you try to find out what's going on?

Day 2

Signs and Symptoms of Anger

When You Can Feel it Coming

ome people get angry very easily. Some might stay angry for days or months, while others can let go of built-up tension through an angry outburst, then simply forget about it and move on—though this doesn't mean those around them can do the same.

Certain people may decide to do nothing about their anger, and instead hold on to it for years, until such a time when they can no longer take it and an angry scene follows. Although many anger-related issues cannot be resolved, the worst thing you can do is let your anger turn into bitterness, be it about life in general or about a particular person or incident.

After an angry outburst, you may feel relieved because you let go of accumulated tension, but it can also make you feel flat, embarrassed, or foolish—not to mention the stress you've created for those who had to witness the scene.

In any case, there are warning signs one is about to "explode." We all learn to recognize these signals from an early age, and continue to perfect the skill as we grow up. Just like we are taught that a dog is getting ready to attack if it flattens its ears, we learn how our parents look or behave when they are mad by watching how they react when they realize we've done something we shouldn't have. Later in life, we learn to interpret the subtle—or not so subtle—signs our partner is about to leave us, or we're about to be laid off.

Being able to pick up vibes from your environment and understand what's going on even when nothing is said is a very useful skill which can sometimes be a real lifesaver.

The tell-tale signs you, or someone else, is about to become angry and possibly dangerous are many, and vary from person to person. However, some of them are common and easy to notice.

16 traits of people prone to anger and/or aggression:

1. They frequently experience road rage.
2. They often blame others for their misfortune.
3. They often feel threatened and believe that others are out to get them.
4. They make scenes when angry.
5. They get angry for even small and insignificant things.
6. They use dominating body language, threats, and screaming to control others.
7. They easily lose their temper.
8. They easily become frustrated.
9. They are unable to control themselves even when they know they'll be sorry later.
10. They have a history of domestic violence.
11. They are in chaotic or problematic relationships.
12. They refuse to accept they have anger issues.

13. They often think or boast about violent confrontations with others.
14. They have been arrested for violence.
15. They drink excessively and are aggressive when drunk.
16. They believe and boast they can easily make others do what they want.

If you know that you or someone close to you is experiencing anger issues, the best thing to do is to explore various anger management techniques which could help not only deal with an explosive temper but understand what it is that makes someone react in such a way.

How Does Being Angry Make You Feel, Look, and Act?

Some people are quick to anger, either because they are short-tempered or because they feel entitled to certain things. Others may need more time to get upset, but their anger may be longer lasting. However, the most problematic type of anger is the kind that leads to physical violence.

Anger is a powerful emotion which affects us on both a physical and emotional level. It not only invokes a strong physiological response, often leading to aggressive and destructive behavior like shouting, thrashing, or violence, it also changes our emotions and encourages certain behaviors we may later not even remember.

<u>Blind rage is particularly common when people are set off for one of these three reasons:</u>

- **Major loss** - For example, a stolen car, a broken-into apartment, or a bag snatched in a restaurant.
- **Grief** - For example, your best friend killed by a drunken driver, your partner cheats on you with someone you trusted.
- **Humiliation** - For example, being belittled in front of others, being insulted because of the way you look, being bypassed for promotion.

While anger can lead to aggression, there's also a positive side to this emotion—it often makes you take steps you might not have otherwise. These steps often lead to change, which does not always have to be external: if you've been bypassed for promotion, you may decide it's time to look for another job, or if your apartment regularly gets broken into, you may decide it's time to improve on security or move to a safer neighborhood.

If you've been angry for years, it may be a sign that something within you needs to change, such as your beliefs, goals, needs, or priorities.

Whether anger will have a negative effect on your life or health, or whether it will prompt you to look deep within and make positive changes in your life, will depend on how honest you are with yourself and how willing you are to embrace change.

Most people who have an anger issue know very well they have a problem, but few decide to do anything about it. If left unaddressed, anger can not only make you a social outcast, but may lead to broken relationships, lost friendships, and even imprisonment.

Anger is like an adrenaline shot which, if not occurring often or allowed to get out of hand, can actually boost your confidence and sense of self-worth. A "dose" of anger, especially if you are fighting for the right cause, can make you feel strong and self-aware.

Just like animals exhibit certain behavior when facing an enemy—dogs raise the fur on their back, cats flatten their ears, horses stamp the ground—people also change their appearance when feeling threatened.

When angry, people may also display some of the behaviors used by many animals. Based on the fight-flight-freeze theory, if they decide they will neither flee nor freeze, but choose to fight, people will often stand tall with slightly spread arms, showing they are ready to fight. They may shout, thrash, or stamp their feet to demonstrate how angry they are, they could become red in the face which makes them look fierce, or they may stare at the opponent or point a finger at him. These body language signals are all part of atavistic behavior, which has helped us survive and which is understood across cultures.

Not only do angry people look threatening, the adrenalin rush makes them feel strong and ready to charge. And when you look and feel threatening, it's easy to go a step further and behave violently.

Physical reaction when feeling angry:

- Increased heart rate
- Increased blood pressure
- Increased breath rate
- Hormonal changes (adrenalin rush)
- Muscles become tense (ready to hit or receive a blow)
- Face becomes red (because of increased blood pressure)

Anger can take different paths and can invoke different emotions, from a desire for physical confrontation to severing communication and withdrawal from the situation or the person you're angry with. However, the physical and emotional manifestations of anger rarely happen at the same time, but are usually spread over a certain period.

How we react to anger depends on our personality, how emotionally intelligent we are, as well as on what caused the anger. Still, certain reactions seem to be common among angry people.

9 stupid and counterproductive things people do when angry:

1. Use bad language
2. Drink excessively
3. Throw or break things
4. Threaten others
5. Refuse to listen
6. Cry
7. Say things they don't mean

8. Behave as if they are entitled to whatever they want
9. Feel proud for demonstrating their strength even over much weaker opponents

So, if you know you're prone to feeling angry, and especially if you often act aggressively, the best thing to do is to start anger management treatment. You can either seek professional help, or you can try to help yourself by reading suitable self-help materials or attending an anger management course.

Anger takes many forms and people deal with it, or struggle with it, in different ways and with different levels of success. However, if you know you've felt angry for a long time, don't assume you're used to it and can continue to deal with it on your own. Bottled-up emotions can change the way you think and behave, even without you realizing it, so it's best to do address it before the accumulated resentment gets you into trouble.

Food for Thought:

How do you usually react when angry? Do you later regret it?

Do you think letting go of bottled up emotions by shouting and screaming at others is okay as long as the person feels less tense afterward?

Some claim that mental or emotional abuse is as bad, or even worse than physical abuse. Do you agree?

Day 3

Why Do I Get Angry?

Many things affect how often you get angry, how long you stay angry, and how you express your anger. Although we all have different anger thresholds, they usually revolve around feelings of personal safety and self-image.

Causes of Anger

Our anger is often based on our interpretation of the situation we find ourselves in. But how we react in a situation also depends on our triggers for anger, which vary from person to person and usually have something to do with our personal boundaries or our view of justice.

4 most common triggers of anger:

1. Feeling threatened

2. Feeling "cornered," helpless, or desperate

3. Feeling you are not being treated fairly

4. Facing injustice (yours or others')

However, we are all different—not everyone may feel threatened, provoked, or mistreated in the same situation. The way we react to challenges has a lot to do with who we are. Our experiences, both those we are currently going through as well as those we went through in the past, affect how we react in a situation, or with people who remind us of something or someone that made us feel unpleasant. The more troubled our life is, the more likely we are to be emotionally unstable, and the greater our need for anger management skills will be.

4 factors that influence your reaction in a challenging situation:

- **Your background**

    If you grew up in a family where it was okay to show your emotions, you will likely continue to be open about your feelings, both positive and negative, as an adult. However, this also means that if you were spoiled as a child and managed to get what you want by throwing tantrums, you will probably continue to exhibit similar behavior throughout life.

    If you were brought up believing that it's rude to complain, chances are you worked out how to swallow your pride and hurt early on. The trouble with this attitude is that unless you later learn how to express your anger, there is a danger you may turn it inward, on yourself.

    And if you witnessed a lot of family violence, you likely grew up believing that anger is a terrifying feeling, and will try to avoid any kind of confrontation for fear of provoking violence.

- **Your past experiences**

  If there are past experiences, like childhood abuse or bullying, that you didn't deal with, you are probably still trying to cope with those feelings of anger even though you may not be aware of it. So, even if you appear happy and confident, deep down, you may still be fighting demons from the past. As a result, you might find certain situations or people difficult to deal with, and if you can't avoid them, being around them is likely to make you feel angry—even though no one would understand why you feel this way.

- **Your current circumstances**

  If you are going through a tough time at the moment, facing a divorce, redundancy, serious health issue, or the loss of a loved one, you are probably not quite yourself. As a result, you probably get angry easily, though you may not understand why.

  If there are situations that you find personally challenging or threatening and you don't address them, the unresolved issue may find an outlet in angry outbursts—which may happen when you least expect it.

  Also, if you are grieving for someone, you may be overwhelmed by conflicting emotions such as sadness, anger, sense of emptiness, guilt, and so on. These contradictory feelings may make it very difficult to cope with otherwise normal challenges, and this may affect how you relate to those you come in contact with. For example, you may snap at others, burst into tears for no reason, or have brief episodes of unexplainable rage.

- **Possible health issues**

  Sometimes, certain health issues may be the cause of anger. According to the mind-body doctrine, our emotions and physical health are very closely linked and depend on each other much more than we realize. Anger can have neurological triggers and if you can't stop feeling angry, or you come to a stage where you wake up feeling angry, you should seek professional help as soon as possible.

  Anger may also be caused by chronic exhaustion. If you are feeling constantly tired, you will have much less energy to do what you're supposed to, or may find it more difficult to concentrate and persevere with your tasks. For these reasons, you'll most likely be less successful in life which, in turn, may make you feel angry with yourself.

Personal Judgment as a Leading Cause of Anger

How we go through life has a lot to do with our mindset—our values, what we see as right or wrong, what we experience as injustice, how cooperative we are, and so on.

Based on this, it makes sense that our own judgment about a situation will decide if we experience it as a threat or injustice. Basically, it is how WE see the world and what WE think is the right reaction to certain triggers and challenges.

It follows that anger, as an emotional response, is about how we experience reality.

So, if you perceive that a situation justifies an angry response, you will act accordingly. This often means that you may decide to take justice into your own hands, which is how many unnecessary confrontations happen.

If you are struggling with anger issues, try to get to a stage where, before you act or react, you can stop for a moment and look at the situation (an argument, provocation, a stupid joke) from a different angle. Try to see it from someone else's eyes. Give the person who is making you angry the benefit of the doubt. What if your judgment is wrong? What if you are overreacting?

We often react based not on facts, but on what we THINK is happening. And what we think is usually influenced by our experiences, culture, and temperament. This is why insight— our ability to have an accurate understanding of a situation or a person—is so important. And so is good judgment, especially when trying to understand what's going on and make the best decision.

However, many studies show that anger does cloud your judgment, which means it's important to calm down before making any big decisions—especially if you know you have a short temper. A recent study published in the academic psychology journal *Intelligence* suggests people prone to anger are also those most likely to overestimate their intelligence, particularly their ability to make good decisions.

Scientists from the University of Warsaw found a link between quick temper and a slightly skewed perception of intelligence. And this is not because these people are not intelligent, but because anger triggers the release of stress hormones that change the way your brain works. In other words, you need to either learn to control your anger or refrain from making any major decisions until you have calmed down.

Food for Thought:

Do you easily get angry? If you do, what are your main triggers? If you don't, how do you control your temper in challenging situations?

1. If memories of how your ex treated you make you "see red," how can you prevent this past hurt from affecting your future relationships? How often do you get angry because something reminds you of a wrong someone has done to you in the past?

2. Do you hate yourself after arguing with someone, or do you pat yourself on the back because you "showed them"?

Day 4

Anger in Children

Just like anger is a perfectly normal emotion in adults, it is equally normal in children. However, there is a major difference between an occasional tantrum or meltdown and prolonged or intense anger outbursts that can lead to ugly scenes or even harm to self or others.

Why Do Children Get Angry?

When anger in children occurs occasionally and passes quickly, we can assume it's part of growing up. But if it becomes an outburst of very intense emotions that last for a long time, it can easily be a mask for an anger-related health disorder.

Dealing with angry children can be difficult, as most parents will testify. Not only is it exhausting both physically and mentally, it sometimes leaves parents feeling guilty or ashamed if they overreacted to a child's misbehavior.

Most people will agree that when they were children, they were not allowed to get away with many of the things children of today expect as their birthright. Today, children are generally more comfortable expressing their emotions, and they also have different expectations of their parents. This shouldn't surprise us—just like we, as adults, have risen our expectations of our governments, employers, or service providers compared to the generation of our parents, so do children of today expect many things and privileges we were not entitled to while we were growing up.

The worst thing a parent can do when facing an angry child is to try to stop him or her from being angry. When you do that, as many parents do, you are forcing your child to suppress their emotions. If the consequence of throwing a tantrum is punishment, a child will quickly learn that anger is something that should not be displayed openly. But this doesn't mean they will stop feeling angry, only that they will stop expressing their emotions for fear of punishment.

Not surprisingly, such children usually grow up into adults who rarely show their feelings. This, in turn, creates many other problems, because bottled-up emotions will sooner or later have to find an outlet. This explains why otherwise perfectly normal, kind, and tolerant people physically or mentally abuse their families, or even get involved in violent crime.

So, rule number one: never try to suppress or ignore the fact that your child is angry, because there is probably a very good reason why he or she feels that way.

6 common reasons why children get angry:

1. **They can't get what they want**

   Children are more intelligent than we give them credit for, and they quickly learn what works and what doesn't. So, if a child is used to being allowed to eat sweets all the time, he or she will react negatively when that favor is withdrawn. Parents often use such favors as a disciplining tool, and if they use it correctly and the child understands that favors are not automatically granted but have to be earned, everything will be fine. However, if a child assumes it is entitled to something which one day becomes unavailable, it will "fight for its rights."

2. **They are teased by peers or adult**

Often, gentle teasing is okay and adults sometimes do it to get children to do something, like saying "I know you can't count to 10" so the child will count to 10 to prove them wrong. However, teasing that makes the child feel embarrassed or stupid can easily provoke angry tantrums.

3. **They react to criticism**

Parents can be extremely demanding, although they believe they do it with the child's best interest in mind. Pushing a child to do something and then criticizing him or her if they fail can make a child angry. However, some children are very spoiled and are not used to criticism—by throwing a tantrum, they are setting boundaries and showing their parents what they can and cannot say.

4. **They are disappointed**

Parents often make promises they have no intention of keeping, just to get a child to do something or stop crying. For a child that has been expecting to be taken to the zoo or given a new toy, this may be a major blow. On the other hand, spoiled children often bully their parents by throwing tantrums until they get what they want.

5. **Disagreement**

This happens sometimes when children are playing with other kids. Children pick up basic social skills during interaction with their peers, but if a child is not used to losing or sharing, being put in a situation where this is required can trigger an angry outburst.

6. **Rejection**

Children, as well as adults with low self-esteem, react intensely to rejection. Being part of a herd is very important to a child, so the reaction to being, or just feeling, rejected by peers or parents may result in hitting, biting, crying, tantrums, or withdrawal.

The easiest way to cope with your child's anger is not to expose them to situations that make them angry. However, this is not always possible, nor would it be a wise thing to do in the long-term. Anger is a part of life, and the best thing you can do for your child is to teach them how to control it.

Some children cope better than others. If your child is prone to anger outbursts, it's best to identify what triggers such behavior and control their exposure to such stimuli, like too much TV, certain games, or the presence of certain children or adults.

If a child takes a long time to stop screaming and tends to become physical when angry, you could be dealing with anger overload. This is not a typical reaction to anger, but is a prolonged outburst where the child is simply inconsolable and unable to stop screaming, crying, or thrashing around.

Anger Management for Kids

To manage anger, you first have to understand what is behind emotional outbursts. Understanding triggers can help you find a solution. In the case of excessive or prolonged anger, you could be dealing with an anger-related disorder. While medication can reduce some of the symptoms of hyperactivity or anxiety, only therapy can provide long-lasting improvement and help keep anger in control.

4 common causes of excessive anger outbursts:

1. Hyperactivity
2. Anxiety
3. Trauma or neglect
4. Health disorders, like learning problems or autism

With young children, "normal" tantrums are common, especially if they feel frustrated or refuse to do something you're asking of them. This is often because very young children can't always explain what they want or how they feel, so they act it out. A tantrum is also the best way to draw attention to oneself, so children often use this as "sign" language to show they are not happy with something.

But sometimes, tantrums happen all the time. If they never seem to stop, or it becomes obvious that a child is unable to control his or her temper, this is usually a sign that you're dealing with a behavior problem.

<u>5 signs that angry outbursts could be a symptom of behavior problem:</u>

1. They don't stop even when the child is older than seven

2. The child's behavior becomes increasingly violent

3. They start getting into trouble at school

4. They can't get along with other kids, so they are often excluded from birthday parties or games.

5. Their behavior starts disrupting family life, like the relationship between parents or with other siblings.

As anger is often the only way a child knows how to react to frustration, parents should take angry outbursts seriously. Instead of telling the child to stop, they should try to figure out what made the child so upset. It is often the feeling of helplessness, quite common in children, that prompts them to express their feelings through anger.

Parents can do a lot to help their children learn how to cope with anger. First of all, they should encourage them to express their emotions, whatever they are, rather than deny them. Secondly, they should find a way of channeling those emotions into something positive. Finding an effective outlet for unexpressed feelings is one of the best ways of preventing them from becoming bottled up.

The reason some children seem to almost enjoy being angry is that an outburst is followed by an adrenaline rush, which boosts their energy. Suddenly, though temporarily, they feel powerful instead of powerless.

But if angry outbursts continue, maybe you as a parent need to reset your own boundaries, adopt a new set of rules, spend more time talking to your child, or take more interest in their life.

Whichever course your child's anger takes, make sure the child understands the difference between anger and aggression. To be angry is okay, being aggressive isn't.

Anger is often a cry for help, especially in very young children who may not be able to clearly explain what bothers them—but even they should be taught how to express their anger in the least harmful way. On the other hand, aggression, especially toward others, should not be tolerated, and this should be made very clear.

Talk to your child as often as you can and try to be aware of what is going on in his or her life, especially outside the home. Prompt them to tell you what is bothering them. To get to a stage where a child will open up, you have to develop a close and trusting relationship.

Don't forget that children copy the behavior of adults, and an excessively angry child may be responding to chaos at home, like alcohol, domestic violence, or abuse.

<u>7 tips on how to deal with an angry child:</u>

1. Praise your child often.

2. Criticize them if you have to.

3. Provide physical outlets.

4. Take an interest in your child's activities—ask about what happened at school, how they like their new teacher, how are their relationships with their peers.

5. Be a role model—if you don't want your child to use bad language or act aggressively, you shouldn't either.

6. Teach children that anger is normal, but that aggression isn't the answer

7. Don't get involved in any conversation as long as the child is screaming. Wait until they have calmed down to find out what has happened.

8. Don't give in to blackmail, but be prepared to listen.

Despite many new approaches to childhood education, discipline is and always will be the key to good behavior. It's about rules and rewards. It's about preventing behavioral problems, and teaching a child what behavior is and isn't acceptable.

As Nicole Ari Parker said, "Raising children is about loving them while trying to figure out how to discipline them."

Food for Thought:

1. Do you think children should get used to receiving criticism, or that they should be spared until they are at least 10 years old? Would too much criticism make them stronger or undermine their ego?

2. Considering their communication skills are limited, do you think children are justified in throwing tantrums? How else could they get adults to do what they want?

3. Think of a relative or a friend who has a child struggling with anger management. What are their parents doing about it? What would you do in their place?

Day 5

Anger in Teens

For a number of physiological, psychological, and social reasons, being a teen is the most difficult period of one's life. When your body is developing from that of a child to that of an adult and your hormones are wreaking havoc in your mind, it's not surprising that you often appear tense and angry.

A teen is but a child in an adult's body—faced with the physical and emotional needs of an adult, but neither fully developed physically and emotionally nor financially independent to be able to fulfill those needs. As a result, they, not surprisingly, often lash out in anger at those they feel are responsible for their unfulfilled needs – their parents.

Why are Teens Angry?

We've all been teenagers before, so we all know how hard growing up can be. In the past, and in some cultures even today, teenagers were more considered to be children than adults. Today, teenagers are—perhaps unfairly—often expected to behave and be responsible for things that normally only adults should deal with.

Handling a child who throws a tantrum can be hard, but it's nothing compared to dealing with an angry and screaming teenager who may be considerably taller and stronger than you.

Teens can be angry with or without reason, and it is up to their parents to curb or fuel that anger. Instead of yelling and fighting back, which may be very tempting but which would only escalate the argument, a parent should try to calm them down.

If you respond to your teen's anger by yelling or threatening, you put yourself on the same level as your child. In some ways, you become equal, which means you lose some of the "weight" at the bargaining table. If this happens, it may be even more difficult to negotiate further. So, whatever you do, don't lose control.

To deal with teen anger, you have to understand what makes them angry. As a parent, you know that although they may try to act like adults, the brains of adolescents are still developing. The way a teen perceives and experiences the world is very different from how an adult sees it, and this should not be used against them.

The problem with angry teens is not that they are often angry for no particular reason, but that they may not be expressing that anger effectively, either because they don't know how to or because they are not allowed to. Unaddressed anger makes people feel powerless and helpless and can sometimes lead to depression or violence—often turned against those who have nothing to do with their feeling of helplessness, but who happen to be an easy target, like pets, siblings, or friends.

The root cause of a teen's anger is usually due to physiological and emotional changes going on in their bodies, as they try to make sense of it. Their social background, as well as the support they get from their families, can either make this process easier or more difficult.

<u>4 things to do when facing an angry teen:</u>

1. Don't use bad language or name-calling, as this will only make things worse.

2. Never make any major decisions, promises, or threats, if you are both in a state. Wait for things to calm down, first. In fact, if both you and your teen are very angry, it's best not to say much. When you have both cooled off, you can address the problem in a more constructive way.

3. Never get physical, because this may easily escalate into violence.

4. Try to listen carefully to what they are saying—their comments or demands may be justified. Even if you don't do anything about it, show you respect them enough to listen to what they have to say. Teenagers

often feel ignored or belittled, and this can be a major anger trigger.

Adolescents are often moody and have strong feelings, which means they often can't think straight nor listen to reason. You shouldn't hold this against them—all the physiological and emotional changes they are going through makes them feel confused and angry.

A teenager's anger is usually directed at those they identify as an obstacle to their desires, which is usually their parents. Other times, they may not be angry with you, but because of something that happened at school or because of an argument with a friend.

Teen Anger Management

Although anger is not bad *per se*, to be used positively, it needs to be managed. There are different ways of expressing anger, and the trick is to express it effectively without hurting others, verbally or physically, or creating an atmosphere of discomfort and fear.

Teens may often seem angry, but are not always sure what or who they are angry with. As a result, they may be prone to snapping or sulking.

However, if a teen stays in this angry mode for months on end, without any particular reason, it could be a sign that their anger had turned inward. Those who sulk for extended periods of time may easily sink into depression, or become violent and start bullying others.

Angry teens can often become rude, asking for trouble, and behaving as if they want to turn every situation into an argument. With such individuals, discussing anything calmly is impossible, and almost any conversation easily spins out of control.

If such behavior becomes frequent, it could be a symptom of an anger-based disorder. Unfortunately, these disorders are particularly common with adolescents who were subjected to physical or mental abuse, or who through TV and video games are often exposed to images of violence, or those who were punished for being angry. Teens who received little or no support while growing up are much more likely to develop some kind of anger-based disorder later in life, simply because they never learned nor were allowed to express their emotions properly.

So, how do you deal with an angry teen? Assuming you understand where their anger is coming from, you will help them the most if you create an environment where they feel safe to express their feelings, regardless of what they are.

Another important thing to do is to try and establish a close relationship with your teen and encourage them to talk to you, so you are more aware of the people they socialize with. The older the teen, the more likely their behavior and values will be influenced by their peers, and peer pressure can lead to inappropriate and destructive behaviors.

10 ways to help teenagers handle their anger:

1. Become a role model on how to manage one's emotions.

2. Allow them to express anger.

3. Never punish them by humiliating them.

4. Be aware of who, outside of the home, may be influencing their behavior.

5. Set rules, but don't forget rewards.

6. Be open to negotiations, but say no to threats, blackmails, and tantrums.

7. Encourage intimacy and bonding, so you know what's going on in their life.

8. Never be too busy to listen to them.

9. Allow them to be open about their feelings.

10. Cultivate mutual trust and respect.

Food for Thought:

1. What were you like as a teen? Were you often angry? If yes, how did you deal with it?

2. When confronted by an angry person, what is the one thing you should never do?

3. When reasoning with an angry teenager doesn't work, how far do you think a teacher or a parent should go

with enforcing discipline? What do you think happens if parents hold different views on how to address their angry teen?

Day 6

Anger as Part of Grief

Just like you can be quietly or ecstatically happy, you can handle your grief with silent sadness or with a massive show of pain and outrage. Regardless of the way you choose to grieve for something or someone (like a way of life or a loved one), anger will definitely play a part in the process.

Why You Should Neither Ignore, Nor Feed Your Anger

There is a legend that one evening. an elderly Cherokee told his grandson about a battle that happens inside every one of us. The battle is between two wolves. One is Evil. It is anger, jealousy, envy, sorrow, regret, greed, arrogance, guilt, resentment, inferiority, self-pity, lies, false pride, superiority, and ego. The other is Good. It is love, joy, peace, hope, serenity, humility, kindness, benevolence, generosity, empathy, truth, compassion, and faith. His grandson thought about this for a short moment, then asked his grandfather, "Which wolf wins?" To this, his grandfather simply replied, "The one you feed."

Emotions are there to be experienced, not bottled up. However, if you experience negative emotions too often or you stay with them for too long, they can eventually become your reality.

Anger, being a very powerful emotion, should not be ignored—it is actually trying to tell you something. Nor should it be fed and nurtured, until it grows beyond control.

Grief is a very personal thing; there is no one-size-fits-all way to grieve. The way you go about it depends on many things, including your support system, your relationship with the deceased, your religion or culture, and your own coping skills. It takes time to get over the loss of a loved one, and although everyone may encourage you to move on with your life, you shouldn't rush through the process—allow it to unfold naturally.

If the crushing sadness makes you feel like you won't be able to go on, or your burning anger at those who could have prevented the death but didn't makes you scream for justice, grief can be frightening. And this is why many people who go through a grieving process end up alone, at the time when they need support the most.

<u>What happens when you ignore anger during grief:</u>

Ignored or unaddressed emotions often come to haunt us later in life. However, Western culture doesn't encourage people to experience overwhelming emotions. Instead, people are encouraged to block or alter them with drugs, divert their attention from what is happening to them with the hypnotic repetition of positive mantras, or simply engage in various feel-good activities.

It's believed that one of the reasons anxiety and depression are increasingly common is that many of our basic feelings are not expressed, but controlled by keeping them swept under the carpet.

If you're dealing with negative emotions, you should try to understand where they're coming from and try to release them. Negative emotions shouldn't be ignored, but nor should you become stuck in them for the rest of your life.

<u>What happens when you feed your anger while grieving:</u>

If, after a personal loss, you dwell on the injustice of it all and cry for revenge, what you are doing is feeding your anger. According to the Law of Attraction, you get more of what you focus on—so by focusing on anger, you attract even more anger and bitterness into your life.

Instead of feeding it, you should starve it and release it.

No matter how frustrated or let down you may feel because of your loss, the faster you stop wallowing in guilt or sorrow, the faster you can get on with your life.

As Ralph Waldo Emerson so wisely pointed out, "A person is what he or she thinks about all day long."

How Anger Helps You Deal with Grief

Anger is often, but not always, part of grief—it's best to think about it as a state in which most of us temporarily find ourselves. Grief can bring feelings of helplessness, regret, blame, or self-blame, and all these emotions can make you very angry. When you hurt, you often try to find someone to blame, which means grieving people often lash out at others.

However, the energy of anger is sometimes directed inward. Some people can start to blame themselves for what happened, or hate themselves for not having been able to do something to prevent the death of their loved one.

10 common recipients of misdirected anger in case of grief:

1. Yourself, for not having done more to prevent the death

2. The person who died, for having abandoned you

3. Surviving family members, or passengers, for not having died instead

4. Doctors, for not having done more to prevent the death

5. Destiny, for leaving you alone, ridden with debt, powerless, or helpless

6. God, for allowing a good person to die

7. Life, for being so unfair

8. The rest of the world, because life goes on as if nothing happened

9. Others, who have not lost what you've lost

10. Everyone who is happy

In that context, being angry is a way of channeling your grieving energy while you try to make sense of your loss. Anger is also usually followed by an adrenaline rush, which boosts your energy levels, giving you the strength to go on.

So, although anger can be painful and frightening, it also represents personal power—which means that it may prompt you to do something to change the situation you are in. And change means action. If anger is expressed positively, it can be channeled into activism, a process that helps release the pain and the feeling of helplessness.

If, on the other hand, you try to suppress your anger—pretending that "that's how it was meant to be," or "it was God's will," or "there was nothing we could have done," while seething with rage and holding onto your anger—the bottled-up emotions may find an outlet in the form of depression or be misdirected to others, like family or friends.

The best way to cope with anger during a grieving process is by acknowledging your pain, your loss, your fears, your despair, and whatever else you may be feeling.

<u>5 ways to cope with anger during grief:</u>

1. Try to understand how you feel about your loss. Stay with the feeling, even if it hurts.

2. If you feel very angry, try to work out who are you angry with and why.

3. Think of ways to rid yourself of anger in a non-destructive way, like through physical exercise, volunteering, writing, or reaching out.

4. If you can't cope with anger because the person who caused your loss got away with it, confront the person you hold responsible for what happened if that's an option you can take, but don't try to escalate the situation.

5. Seek professional help if you find it hard to go on.

Finally, to be able to grieve and deal with the anger that often accompanies it, you have to understand the six stages of grief that you'll be going through.

<u>6 stages of grief:</u>

- **Shock**

   This is how your mind tries to protect you from overwhelming pain: "What? No, it can't be!"

- **Denial**

  This is how your mind tries to protect you from reality: "No, it can't be true."

- **Anger**

  This is when you start grieving in earnest when the truth finally hits you: "Why? Why me?"

- **Guilt**

  You will sooner or later start lamenting why you hadn't done more to prevent your loss: "If only I'd been there, maybe he'd still be alive."

- **Pain and sorrow**

  This is the hardest and most frightening part of the grieving process, because by then, you are fully aware of what has happened and you are forced to face reality.

- **Release and resolution**

  This is the stage of grief where you start accepting the reality and getting ready to let go of the relationship.

However, having gone through all six stages does not mean you're over your grief. It will continue to come back and haunt you from time to time—to prevent this from happening, it's very important to deal with the pain and close this chapter of your life.

To heal, it's important to go through all the stages of grieving. Then, you can accept the reality, forgive yourself and others, and move on.

Food for Thought:

1. Think of a painful memory you can't get out of your head. Do you realize that by thinking about it continually, you are feeding your anger? What would it take to release it? Why would anyone enjoy wallowing in self-pity?

2. Think of a time when you lost someone. How did you deal with the loss? What was the prevailing emotion— anger or sadness?

3. When a loved one has a life-threatening disease, it gives everyone time to prepare for their departure. On the other hand, when someone dies in a car accident, it comes as a major shock. Which scenario causes more anger?

Day 7

How Anger Affects Relationships

Chronic anger has a devastating effect on relationships—not only because it destroys love and trust, but because it creates a toxic and often unsafe atmosphere at home. Just like gathering clouds can warn us of an approaching storm, chronic anger issues are often a sign of an accident waiting to happen.

Anger as a Medley of Emotions

Anger is a complex emotion and unless it is managed, can be devastating to your health, relationships, and career. If you have an anger problem, it's important to work on it when you are NOT feeling angry, instead of waiting for an angry reaction to try and find the best ways to deal with it.

However, anger doesn't appear out of the blue—it is a response to another emotion or particular triggers.

Just like happiness is contagious, so is anger. When you are angry, it spills over to your environment, even if you aren't making a scene. Those around you can pick up on your quiet anger and, depending on their relationship with you, may feel intimidated or simply uncomfortable in your company. As a result, they may start avoiding you.

Although people in your environment—be it your family, colleagues, or friends—may have nothing to do with the reason you're angry, they often find themselves the target of your anger. You may snap at them, be sarcastic, or openly lash out. And this is what ruins many relationships.

When you start taking your anger out on others, especially if they are in no position to respond or physically remove themselves from you, your anger becomes a sort of bullying. If you know this is happening, the first thing you need to do is acknowledge that you have an anger problem which is getting out of control.

The best way to deal with a chronic anger issue in a relationship is to address the real cause; however, how you approach this will depend on who is having the problem.

If YOU have an anger problem:

- Look for a solution to this problem cool-headed. In other words, calm down first so you can think clearly. Anger releases certain hormones in our brain which can affect the decision-making process.

- Acknowledge your uncontrolled anger is creating problems in the relationship.

- Dig deep and try to understand why you feel so angry. It may have nothing to do with your partner, so why are you taking it out on them?

- Discuss your anger with your partner. Ask them how they feel during your outbursts. Try to see yourself through your partner's eyes and understand how this has been affecting your relationship.

- Together, make a plan for how you can start managing your anger. If nothing else, promise yourself you will refrain communicating with your partner or making any major decisions when overwhelmed with frustration, fear, or rage. Chances are, you will say or do things you'll regret later.

If YOUR PARTNER has an anger problem:

- Help him or her calm down when they are in a state.

- Listen to what they have to say, even if you don't agree with them. Let them speak. Even when people have every reason to feel angry, they will often vent their anger while talking about it, so confrontation is avoided.

- Communication is key for healthy relationships—the more you talk to each other, the less likely you are to have communication problems.

If BOTH PARTNERS have an anger problem:

- Dealing with an angry partner is bad enough, but if both suffer from chronic anger problems, the relationship usually would not work. Especially if neither is used to apologizing, staying calm during an argument, listening, or accepting another's point of view.

Psychologists believe that the main problem with anger is what we do with it—do we manage it, do we ignore it, do we direct it toward others or toward ourselves?

Unfortunately, uncontrolled anger often leads to fighting, blaming, name-calling, or bringing up the past. The more of these things you do to your partner when you're angry, the more difficult it becomes to go back to normal once you've calmed down, for some words or actions cannot be taken back.

We know that anger often goes hand in hand with other emotions, like feeling ashamed, hurt, or frightened. According to psychologists, anger is like an iceberg—only 10% of it shows while the remaining 90%, which is unseen, is what really is making you angry. So, while to others you may appear angry, what you are actually feeling is fear, shame, hurt, and more. Find out what your submerged iceberg is made out of.

During an argument, an angry person will often criticize their partner, which is counterproductive.

Here are 5 signs you're dealing with anger in your relationship the wrong way:

- If you are criticizing the character, rather than the behavior of your partner.

- If the criticism is supposed to make them feel guilty.

- If you are not doing this to improve your relationship, but just trying to let go of your bottled-up tension— criticizing them just to make yourself feel better, regardless of how the criticism is making your partner feel.

- If you refuse to listen to what your partner has to say in their defense, but expect them to do as you say.

- If your criticism is insulting or belittling.

Misplaced Anger

hile anger is important, because it often tells us in no uncertain terms that something needs to change, it can also be a destructive emotion.

We live in a stressful and often very unfair world, and not everyone copes well with pressure. When dealing with everything they have on their plate proves too much, some people simply lose it.

Unfortunately, those who find themselves at the receiving end of their angry outbursts are usually not those who caused it, but those they have access to. In most cases, this is a family member.

While one way of managing anger is to make sure you find a positive outlet for your emotions, misplaced anger will easily destroy a relationship, especially if it happens repeatedly.

5 causes of misplaced anger

1. **Suppressed anger**

   As many a wife will testify, women often find themselves on the receiving end of their frustrated husband's emotions. Although talking to your spouse is a great way to relieve tension and frustration, it has to be done in a way that is not harmful. In other words, you shouldn't destress by stressing someone else out.

2. **Desperation**

   Regardless of what it is you feel hopeless about, depending on your nature, you may sink into depression, make scenes, or lash out in indignation.

3. **Not taking time-off**

   The more stress in your life you have to cope with, be it at work or at home, the more you need to take care of your mental health. If you can't afford vacations, at least take weekends off from time to time. The best way to unwind is to get involved in something that makes you happy—that's what hobbies are for.

4. **Negative mindset**

Some people find it very difficult to see anything positive in any situation. Instead, they   dwell on problems (both real and imaginary), wants, lacks, or potential disasters (theirs or global). Not only will this attitude make you feel miserable all the time, it will probably also make you very angry.

5. **Resentment**

We all feel resentful from time to time, but if this emotion lasts for very long, it can become part of your character. This usually has to do with some injustice done to you, but instead of addressing it, some people choose to wallow in pain and bitterness for the rest of their lives.

The worst thing is that many people are fully aware that their anger is misplaced, but can't or won't do anything about it. For how long your partner will be able to put up with it depends on many things, but even if you are not aggressive when you're angry, misplaced anger is very toxic for a relationship.

5 reasons misplaced anger destroys a relationship:

- It creates a negative atmosphere at home.
- Angry outbursts are unpleasant, disrespectful, and unsettling.

- It's very belittling to be treated like a doormat.

- Chronically angry individuals are difficult to live with because you never know when the next outburst is coming.

- Such people may not be safe to live with, especially if they have a history of aggression.

Food for Thought:

1. What do you do when you feel your partner or friend is angry about something? Do you try to distract them from what's bothering them, or do you get them to talk about it?

2. Some people go for a drink after work so they can relax and diffuse their accumulated   tension in order not to pass it on to their family. Others expect their partners to help them unwind, although it usually means they will have to listen to the well-known complaints, objections, or dramas. Which approach do you think is better?

3. If you often have to suppress your anger, how do you make sure it doesn't become bottled up?

Day 8

Anger in the Workplace

Although there are many reasons to get angry, in a private situation—with family or friends—you can say things or even behave in an inappropriate way and still be forgiven. In the workplace, however, the situation is very different. While you and your sibling or spouse may fight regularly and still love each other, if you scream at your colleagues, call them names, or shame them, you are likely to get fired. Most people know this and try to control their temper at work as much as they can, but, this can lead to the most common cause of anger in the workplace—frustration.

Why is the Workplace Anger so Common?

Frustration is the main cause of anger in the workplace. However, what lies behind this frustration is often that these people know that, for one reason or another, they have to remain in the job (or organization) they do not enjoy. This creates resentment, which is a form of long-lasting unresolved anger.

6 reasons people feel frustrated in the workplace:

1. Being passed over for promotion.

2. Having to do what you are told even if you know it won't work.

3. Having to report to a much younger or less intelligent person.

4. Having to report to women (in some cultures, this would be a major blow to many men).

5. Having to work after hours or on weekends with no pay (this is common in organizations planning for layoffs, where many people try to make themselves irreplaceable by showing they are willing to work extra hours for no pay).

6. Having to take the blame for your boss' wrong decisions.

Most employers would rather not employ frustrated employees—they are rarely motivated enough to achieve good results, and can be a potential threat to the organization if they start lobbying against the management.

For you, however, long-held frustration can be a major threat to your health. If unaddressed, the simmering bitterness can lead to burnout, heart disease, high blood pressure, stroke, depression, or other conditions.

And the more you feel you are stuck in your position, the more frustrated you'll feel. If, due to your age or lack of skills, you know you are unlikely to find a better job and know you have to stay with the one you're currently in, or if there are not many jobs available where you live, or if the pay is good, you may feel trapped in a job you hate or with people you have no respect for.

The causes of frustration in the workplace are too numerous to list, but they usually revolve around some kind of a disappointment, like a poor performance evaluation, unfair treatment, being micromanaged, or being criticized too often.

However, disappointment may also be caused by unrealistic expectations. Maybe you assumed you'd be promoted in two years, or that you'd be given a car to go with the job.

The reason you appear angry at work may also have nothing to do with the workplace. If you have a troubled or chaotic personal life, it is likely to affect your professional life, as well—the frustration one brings from home is often directed at one's colleagues. This is a typical example of misplaced anger of browbeaten wives and husbands.

Whatever the cause of your anger in the workplace might be, you have to try and manage it as best you can. Mild irritation is what we all learn to deal with, however, if something happened that made you see red and you feel you're about to make a scene—stop.

<u>8 things to do if you get very angry at work:</u>

1. Take a deep breath or several deep breaths

2. Slowly count to ten

3. Tell yourself to stay calm

4. Try to prevent tension in your muscles, jaw, head, or stomach. Keep breathing and try to loosen your muscles.

5. Walk away from your desk

6. Get out of your office or the building

7. Take a short walk, call a friend, or chat to a colleague you can trust

8. When you have calmed down, think through how to address the problem that made you so mad

How to Deal with Work-Related Anger if You're a Manager

An organization where anger seems to be present all the time is not a nice place to work in. It could be a major HR issue that's making staff unhappy, or just one or two people who, for their own reasons, enjoy stirring things up.

Try to find out who or what is behind this underlying anger. Consider the office safety regulations first, to make sure personal safety is not what's making employees lack focus or drive.

Some problems you may be able to deal with on your own, but in case of major issues, it's best to get professional help, lest things get out of control. Hiring an external consultant to talk to staff often helps, for they may feel less intimidated approaching someone outside of the company.

There may be situations when you have to make unpopular decisions, like redundancies, pay cuts, benefits withdrawal, and so on; however, a negative atmosphere in a company is usually a result of the prevailing culture. Although problematic individuals have to be dealt with, keep in mind that overall dissatisfaction easily turns into anger.

If anger prevails and you can't figure out what may be the cause, perhaps you need to look at this problem from different angles. If it turns out that certain individuals are causing trouble and raising tension (or expectations), it could be that stress from their private lives is spilling over to their work environment. While there is usually not much you can do about their personal problems, you can at least talk to them to see if there is anything you can do to help make things easier at work.

Anger is the workplace can be very difficult to deal with, and many managers turn a blind eye or postpone taking any action for as long as they can. As a manager, though, you must be mentally and emotionally prepared to take action, taking care not to overreact or underreact.

10 things a manager can do to help employees deal with anger in the workplace:

1. Create a professional workplace culture of tolerance and mutual respect.

2. Set rules and expectations and make sure all new employees are aware of them.

3. Encourage communication and, if possible, organize communication training for staff on a regular basis.

4. Be approachable.

5. Provide anger management training, which would show people how to deal with their anger and how to respond to angry colleagues.

6. Deal with inappropriate behavior as soon as possible. The longer you put off an unpleasant confrontation, the more likely it is to get out of hand.

7. Employees with anger issues can create an unhealthy atmosphere in the company they work for, so recommend anger management treatment or fire them.

8. Keep written records of such incidents.

9. Have a zero-tolerance policy in the case of aggressive behavior.

10. In case of major problems, always consult an attorney or an HR professional.

Food for Thought:

1. What do you find most frustrating in your workplace? Is that something beyond your control, or can you do something about it?

2. Were you ever in a situation at work where you took part in an argument you now feel embarrassed about? What happened to make you react like that? How would you deal in the same situation today?

3. If you were a manager and had to fire your best employee for sexual harassment to protect a temp who only started working two months ago, what would you do?

Day 9

Anger-Related Disorders

You may have an anger problem because of a health disorder you are struggling with, or you can develop a health disorder because of a long-standing unaddressed anger problem. In the modern world, anger-related health issues are becoming very common. It seems that as the world gets faster, the people get angrier. Anger can often lead to other negative emotions, like resentment, hatred, self-pity, fear, or aggression, and over time, these self-destructive feelings can turn into disease or illness.

How Anger Affects Your Health

People with chronic anger problems are often those who remain stuck in an injustice (real or imaginary) that has befallen them. There may be a very good reason why someone is angry, but for this emotion to be constructive rather than destructive, it has to be managed.

Unfortunately, many people accept injustice as part of their fate or karma, and live their entire lives feeling angry and bitter. Others, because they can't accept the situation but don't know how to deal with it, become irritable and aggressive. There are also those who are simply short-tempered, and their anger can be triggered by almost anything.

Although many situations are beyond your control, what you do have control over is the way you react. Unless you exert this control, the uncontrolled angry episodes can sap your energy and health very quickly.

We know being angry is not healthy, but it was only relatively recently that the World Health Organization recognized 32 disorders as directly linked to dysfunctional anger, the best-known ones of which are:

- **Intermittent Explosive Disorder**

  Individuals with this disorder display "the degree of aggressiveness which is grossly out of proportion to any provocation or precipitating psychosocial stressor." This disorder is believed to be behind most mass shootings. The strange thing is that most of these individuals don't have a prior history of aggressive behavior. Typically, they are normal, polite, and friendly people. Then, all of a sudden, a rejection or a stressful event pushes them to a breaking point, and they go on a rampage. Their action is supposed to "restore honor or repay the injury."

- **Oppositional Defiant Disorder**

  This disorder manifests as defiance and anger against authority, and is most common in children and adolescents. However, this is not a case of occasional frustration or disobedience. These individuals have frequent tantrums, refuse to comply, argue excessively, blame others for their mistakes, behave rebelliously, and are often vindictive.

What makes the diagnosis of anger-related disorders particularly difficult is that they often appear alongside another emotional problem. This means that if you see a therapist to seek treatment for anger, the real reason for your emotional dysfunction may be another disorder you are probably not even aware of, and it's this that makes diagnosis and treatment difficult.

Anger affects various processes in your body—digestion, assimilation, cell production, circulation, healing, immune system, and more. As a result, if anger persists for months or years, it's very likely to weaken your immune system and to directly or indirectly lead to a number of problems:

- Headaches
- Digestion problems
- Insomnia
- Anxiety
- Depression
- High blood pressure
- Heart attack
- Stroke
- Skin problems

The Most Common Anger Disorders

Anger becomes disordered if the individual exhibits pathological aggressive, violent, or self-destructive behaviors which are driven by chronically repressed anger. Fortunately, most of us figure out how to manage our anger, so anger disorders are likely to happen only to those whose anger was not only not managed, but was repressed for a long time.

Another cause of anger disorder is neurological dysfunction and substance abuse, which both affect the way we control our violent impulses.

6 most common forms anger can take:

1. **Chronic anger**

   This is anger which has lasted for a long time. It usually has a major effect on our immune system and may be the cause of other mental disorders.

2. **Passive anger**

   This type of anger is difficult to identify, because it does not have typical anger symptoms.

3. **Overwhelmed anger**

   This kind of anger happens if there is too much going on in your life, and you can neither do something about it nor can you cope anymore. In other words, this happens when you feel overwhelmed with life.

4. Self-inflicted anger

This type of anger is usually the result of feelings of guilt, shame, or self-blame. It is directed inward and can be very self-destructive.

5. Judgmental anger

This type of anger is common in people who are resentful about a situation or life in general.

6. Volatile anger

With this type of anger, individuals find it hard to control themselves and often display aggressive behavior.

Anger management techniques can help you keep many of the anger-related health disorders under control, and studying anger management materials such as this one can help you understand what you're dealing with.

8 ways anger management helps you deal with your anger:

1. Teaches you about anger and how to use it positively
2. Helps you understand your anger and identify your anger triggers
3. Suggests ways of reacting in such situations
4. Shows you how to relax and defuse anger

5. Helps you identify thoughts and beliefs associated with anger

6. Shows you why dwelling on past problems or hurts is counterproductive

7. Helps you resolve conflicts

8. Helps you identify alternatives to revenge

Food for Thought:

1. Do you know someone with a health disorder? How do you feel in their company? How do you think they feel in yours?

2. Discuss three situations where having anger management skills would help you resolve conflict more professionally.

Day 10

Anger Across Cultures

How you react to anger depends on many things, including your age, gender, and circumstances. However, the definition of anger, and especially of what justifies angry behavior, is largely based on the culture one comes from. In some cultures, expressing your emotions—particularly anger—may be considered very ill-mannered, other cultures encourage people to openly demonstrate how they feel about something. So, while many may consider people from the East as stony-faced and emotionless, to Asians, Westerners probably seem very rude.

Cultural Norms and Emotions

Anger has many definitions, causes, and possible outlets. It is often associated with hurt feelings, frustration, and a desire for justice or revenge. However, as cultures hold different attitudes toward anger, local norms will either encourage or curb angry displays in public.

Comparative studies on the way children are brought up show that in China (as well as throughout the Far East) demonstrating emotions is curbed in children from an early age. Tantrums are usually ignored, and children are left to cry until they have calmed down. Considering their cultural values, this is necessary for a child to develop socially-acceptable behavior.

In many Eastern cultures— Chinese, Japanese, Thai—anger is something that is usually not discussed, especially not in public. Children are discouraged to mention it, e.g., complain about something, or are punished if they do.

In Western culture, however, parents usually fuss and fret over their children, particularly during their fits of anger.

Cultural norms also influence how much anger is considered normal for a man and how much for a woman. In most patriarchal societies, girls are raised not to show their emotions openly—particularly negative ones such as anger. Although things have changed a lot in the last 200 years, in the West, public display of anger is discouraged in girls even today.

On the other hand, boys were, in a way, expected to show a certain degree of assertiveness (often manifested as an angry or aggressive behavior). If they didn't, they were believed not to have the necessary confidence to succeed in life.

Still, in most cultures, boys' anger is tolerated much more than that of girls, even when it leads to aggressive behavior—anger is believed to be what distinguishes them from the feminine characteristics of being kind, quiet, and forgiving.

Display of Emotions in Public

Despite the fact that in the West, anger—especially if it leads to aggression—is discouraged and sanctioned, there is still a disproportionately high level of anger among children. Many believe that it is TV and Internet games behind most of the unhealthy behaviors.

But even very young children seem to show signs of anger and aggressiveness toward others, as we can see with school bullying. For this reason, in the West, everyone is encouraged to talk about their anger problems so they can be addressed and channeled on time—especially children.

Until relatively recently, social status played a major part in how much someone was allowed to express anger. In the West, it was generally believed that the lower classes exhibited more anger—likely because, due to their socio-economic condition, they had more reason to be angry.

In Japan, however, it was those of a higher social status who exhibited more anger, as a symbol of their authority. So, although the display of anger was generally considered very rude and was sanctioned, it was granted only to those who felt entitled to almost anything because of their social status.

While most American citizens don't refrain from expressing anger in public, including making a major scene if they're angry, people in the Far East tend to avoid conflict at all costs. Regardless of how they may really feel—angry, embarrassed, or sad—they will smile. However, this "happy face" is the result of lifelong social conditioning and does not mean they actually feel happy or relaxed.

Cultural norms dictate what is and what isn't allowed, and serve as a guide to socially-acceptable behavior. Western and Eastern cultures approach anger problems in completely different ways. In Western culture, people are encouraged to openly show positive emotions, and manage the display of negative ones, but they are still allowed to express them. In Eastern cultures, people opt for the "middle way" (i.e., Tao), constantly seeking a balance between positive and negative emotions.

They start instilling these values into their children as early as preschool, which means American and Asian children have different reactions to visual stimuli. While in Europe and America, children prefer exciting activities, cartoons, or comics, in the Far East, they prefer calm emotions—smiles instead of laughter, not overly competitive games, or not very excitable stories.

Additionally, while American parents will use every available opportunity to boost their children's confidence, Chinese parents are more likely to downplay their children's good results so as not to inflate their ego.

Finally, bestsellers in America contain much more excited and arousing content when compared to bestsellers in Asia. So, although many believe that we now live in a global village and that our cultures are merging into one, when you dig a little deeper, it becomes obvious that cultural differences are still very present, although often skillfully disguised.

PART 2

Anger Management

Day 11

When Anger Becomes a Problem

While expressing anger is okay, and is actually good for your health, if you do it inappropriately or start feeling it too intensely or too often, it stops being a normal emotion and becomes a problem.

During an angry outburst, your body produces certain hormones. If these are released too frequently or for too long, they negatively affect your health in a number of ways.

So, while releasing anger is an important part of your mental health, this only works if you do so in a way that does not jeopardize your physical health or alienate you from society.

The Primitive Brain

Anger often becomes a problem when your body and mind are not in alignment. Your reaction during a fight-flight-freeze situation is a remnant of atavistic behavior, which was important when we lived close to nature—and still is, for those who continue to live that way.

However, over the past 30,000 years, our bodies and our environment didn't change at the same rate. While our bodies and instincts remained the same as those of a caveman, our physical and social environments changed beyond recognition.

In the 21st century, we are no longer regularly exposed to dangers that would make the fight-flight-freeze instincts necessary for our survival. However, to survive the stress, constant change, and fast pace of the modern world, we now need a very different set of skills—and anger management is one of them.

Numerous studies on the importance of the brain in human development show that the so-called "primitive brain"—the part of the brain that concerns our survival instincts—is much more powerful and important than the part responsible for our cognitive abilities.

The studies show that regardless of how much control we try to exercise over the neocortex part of the brain—no matter how much we try to stick to morals, ethics, and good intentions—when we find ourselves in a life-threatening situation, the primitive part of our brain, the part dealing with instincts, takes over. This, according to neuroscience, explains why we so easily become overcome by rage or fear and are unable to stop it.

This means that although our bodies have remained, from an evolutionary perspective, similar to that of a caveman's, our minds "moved on" and continued to develop and adapt to the changed environment and circumstances.

For this reason, there is often a clash between what we think we should do and what we actually do. As our body's reaction didn't change in face of danger (not only physical danger), the saying "do what you feel is right" makes a lot of sense. However, although your body and your instincts may know what's best for you, you may not be able to act on it. Our world requires that we stick to laws, rules, and cultural norms which often go against our instincts.

Although the world has changed a lot, it doesn't mean we face fewer dangers today than we did all those years ago. The main difference is that the dangers of today don't come from our physical environment, like wild animals, hostile tribes, or starvation, but from our lifestyle.

5 main "dangers" we face today:

1. Chronic stress
2. Overpopulation and lack of personal space
3. Competitiveness
4. Fast living
5. The fast-changing world

As our physical bodies failed to change at the same rate with which our social environment has changed, our reactions to the stress and tension of the modern times is simply the result of our bodies trying to cope with the circumstances for which they were not designed. Therefore, the primitive parts of our brains react to these stressors the same way they would to an imminent attack by a wild animal or any other physical danger.

Unfortunately, not everyone copes well with stress. These stressors, especially if they happen too often or remain unaddressed, often make us angry.

As a species, we are faced with 4 major problems:

- Adapting to an environment that is changing much too fast
- Developing unhealthy lifestyles to match the changing environment
- Coping with stress
- Dealing with anger issues which often result from the stress the world seems to be drowning in

So, does this mean our primitive brain is why so many of us seem to be so angry all the time? Probably not. Our brains are simply trying to help us survive in the face of the threats we face, regardless of what they are. It does not distinguish between a hungry wolf about to attack and an angry boss who threatens to fire you. In both scenarios, you're in serious trouble, and the adrenaline rush is simply there to help you make the best decision under the circumstances and save your life or job.

However, we live in a sophisticated world and even if you are provoked and feel very angry, you should try to control your reactions.

Intense anger can lead to violence, which can result in physical injury, imprisonment, or even loss of life. Even if your anger does not lead to violence, if you express it inappropriately, your position in society may be seriously damaged. Violent and rude people can easily become social outcasts.

If you are known for your temper, others may feel intimidated in your presence and start avoiding you, refusing to have anything to do with your family, or preventing their children from socializing with yours. A poorly-managed temper may cost you your relationship, job, and health.

There are people who act angrily and aggressively not because they can't control their primitive brain, but because they feel good when they are intimidating others. Some may believe people are more likely to listen or respect them that way. Others may act aggressively because they never learned how to manage their anger and simply don't know a better way to express annoyance, resentment, or pain. When someone has been under significant pressure for a long time, they may no longer care how their angry outburst make others feel as long as they release the accumulated tension.

Another problem with anger is that it can become a habit. And as breaking a habit requires determination and perseverance, you may find it easier to stick to your routine rather than try to change it.

If you're struggling with anger, perhaps you should consider anger management counseling, where you can learn how to process it and release it in a way that is neither self-destructive nor harmful to your environment.

Can the Primitive Brain be Controlled?

Being unable to adapt to a changing environment is what's believed to have exterminated the dinosaurs. So, to avoid getting into trouble because of anger—yours or someone else's—you should learn to recognize the first physical signs of the emotion.

<u>7 early signs of anger:</u>

1. Tension in the shoulders
2. Headache
3. Foot tapping
4. Fast heart rate
5. Short breaths
6. Sweating
7. Facial flushing

What these physiological changes mean is that your body is telling you to get ready for action—maybe facing an angry client, being wrongfully accused of something you didn't do, or a possible animal attack.

It's crucial that at this stage you calm yourself down, before you say or do anything. The greater the danger, the more careful you have to be with how you'll react.

- Try to breathe more slowly and concentrate on your breath.
- Try to think what the best way is to resolve the issue.
- If the person facing you is angrier than you are, try to calm them down. Let them say what they have to say and try to get them to talk it over.

- It will help if you haven't used any alcohol or drugs prior to the incident, as both tend to lower inhibition and offer a false sense of power. Most angry and aggressive outbursts happen when alcohol is involved. So, if you're anticipating an unpleasant meeting, don't have a drink to brace yourself for the encounter. All you will achieve is a boost to your ego, which may cost you dearly.

- If you are not in imminent danger, when you've calmed down and hopefully lowered your blood pressure, try to talk yourself into a sensible solution. Alternatively, try to think about something positive.

However, this comes easier to some people than others. If you have a problem controlling your emotions and tend to overreact to provocations, injustices, or stress, it's time to consider anger management treatment.

So, although our instincts often help us get out of a sticky situation, we do need to adapt our behavior to the world we live in. If you know you have an anger problem, learning about anger management can help you understand where your emotions are coming from and how best to express them. However, there are some simple things you can do, starting from today, that will make you less prone to rash behavior or overreaction.

3 simple ways of taming your temper:

1. **Physical exercise**

If you lead a very stressful life, or for some reason often find yourself in situations or with people who provoke an angry reaction in you, you should make physical exercise an essential part of your life, as it will help you release tension.

Well-known psychologist V Schutt believes exercise helps dissolve anger because it helps you channel your emotions. Scientists are still not sure how this happens, but believe it has something to do with the way physical exercise affects the serotonin levels in the brain, which help regulate behavior. Physical exercise is particularly important for those who have aggressive tendencies.

2. **Mindfulness**

If you are used to tuning in to your emotions, perhaps mindfulness can help you understand why you feel and react the way you do. When you feel angry, how does your body react—what happens in your chest, face, heart, stomach? How do you feel— exploited, helpless, abandoned—and why? What are the thoughts that go through your head?

When you have calmed down, try to discuss the incident that made you angry with the person involved. Try not to start with accusations, but by explaining how the incident made you feel.

Being mindful about your anger is about admitting to yourself that you're not coping well, but also that you don't want to ignore your negative emotions—you want to do something about them. Anger management can be a difficult and long process, so be patient with yourself.

3. Meditation

Meditation is an easy and simple way of preventing anger from getting out of control. Although there are many different ways to meditate, all revolve around self-awareness.

The practice of meditation helps you recognize the signs of anger, so you can learn how to react when you notice anger building up.

In other words, meditation improves your self-control and ability to calm your mind by focusing on something positive. If you practice it daily, you will soon become calmer and less stressed out, which will indirectly change the way you react to anger-provoking situations.

Meditation has been successfully used to deal with problematic adolescents and even in the rehabilitation of violent criminals.

Day 12

Handling Emotions

There is a proverb that "a man without self-control is like a city broken into and left without walls."

Emotions, both positive and negative, are a normal part of our lives—provided they are kept under control. Emotions help us understand how we feel about something or someone, like whether we can relax or should be on our guard, whether we can count on someone or not, how self-confident we should feel under the circumstances, and so on.

Still, we shouldn't allow our feelings to rule our lives, but should aim to take charge of them and rule them, instead. And this only happens if you know how to handle your emotions.

How to Take Charge of Your Emotions

Most of us know, sometimes subconsciously, what sort of situations or individuals push our buttons. And, if we give it some thought, we can better prepare ourselves to face emotionally-charged situations or difficult people ahead of time.

Just like how you prepare for an important meeting or an interview, if you know that finding yourself around certain people or in a certain situation is likely to make you feel angry and act inappropriately, work on bracing yourself for the event.

You can do this by preparing yourself mentally and emotionally for what you think is likely to happen. That way, since you have a better idea of what to expect, you'll be ready to deal with those challenges in a positive and constructive manner.

When you take charge of your emotions, you can prevent the situation from getting out of hand. This is particularly important for situations which are likely to escalate and for those who know they have an anger problem.

So, assuming you find it hard to control your temper or often find yourself in situations which make you behave inappropriately, you should prepare an Action Plan for handling your emotions.

8 things to do when you want to improve the way you handle your emotions:

1. Avoid if you can

Whenever possible, try to avoid the situations and people that are likely to make you angry. Unfortunately, this is often not possible, and all you can do is hope to have enough time to prepare mentally and emotionally before confronting them.

2. Emotions are a matter of choice

With a healthy dose of self-control and emotional intelligence, it's easy to avoid getting angry—even in the company of those who easily push your buttons. Being able to handle your emotions is about taking full control of how you react to anger triggers.

3. Try to make the situation less tense

It's often possible to defuse the tension if you make a conscious effort to do so. For example, if you know that a friend is touchy about certain issues, avoid discussing them. If your boss is particular about punctuality, make an effort to get to work on time. We often do things we know irritate others either because we're too lazy to make an effort, because we enjoy pushing their buttons, or because we are so self-centered we simply don't think about how what we say may make others feel.

4. Ask yourself why certain individuals or situations trigger such an angry response in you

Sometimes, when you are angry with others, you may actually be angry with yourself. It's not uncommon to project what we feel about ourselves onto others. For example, if someone's arrogance makes you angry, are you sure it's not because you reserve arrogance for yourself and are annoyed that someone else is behaving the way you think YOU are entitled to act?

We often say to others what we should be saying to ourselves—"Don't be so impatient," "Why are you so selfish?" So, the saying "It takes one to know one" makes a lot of sense.

5. Try to ignore the triggers

If you know that in certain situations you always get angry, try to shift your focus. For example, if you find the way someone dresses irritating, try to shift the focus from their clothing style to other aspects of their personality, like their work ethics or their empathy. It's easy to get angry if you focus on what you don't like or disapprove of.

6. Change your thoughts

If you can control your thoughts and attitudes, you'll have no problem controlling your emotions—your thoughts create your emotions. When you stop focusing on the negative in your life, such as rude colleagues, unfair working conditions, family struggles, or the consequences of environmental pollution, you will automatically feel less angry. And if you get to a stage where you can feel genuinely happy for others, you will become less judgmental, more compassionate, and will rarely feel angry.

7. Change your reaction

Changing the way you react to a trigger is not easy—it's something you have to work on all your life. However, when you can control your emotions, you have control over your life. By making an effort to choose your response to a trigger, you are taking control of a potentially chaotic situation. It's well-known that anger breeds anger—when you choose to react angrily, be prepared to receive a similar reaction from others.

8. Focus on the solution, not the problem

Instead of constantly thinking about how horrible the people you work with are, try to either change them, change yourself, accept the situation, or find another job. By focusing on the negative in your life, like a disloyal friend, a dead-end relationship, a low-paying job, failing health, you are making yourself bitter and irritable. Wallowing in self-pity and anger can't bring you anything good, so why do it? Why not try to find a solution to your problem, instead of ruminating about the unfairness of life?

How to Control Angry Emotions

We can usually see an angry reaction coming, like when the meeting is not going in the right direction or when we know in advance that a particular situation is likely to turn nasty. This means we usually have time to prepare ourselves for situations which we suspect may provoke an angry reaction, either in us or in others.

If you want to be the master of your life and you know you have an anger problem, try to adopt practices which can help you control both the anger triggers and your reaction to those triggers.

6 habits that can help you control your emotions in any situation:

1. Tune into your inner self

This is a very useful exercise, particularly when you're feeling unhappy, upset, or angry. Start by asking yourself why you are feeling that way. Pay attention to any emotions or thoughts that come up—sadness, anxiety, envy, rage, and so on.

Tuning in is about being in touch with your innermost feelings. It's about reconnecting with your intuition. Most of us have been encouraged not to rely on our gut feelings, but to base our decisions on our logical minds.

Listening to your intuition in the noisy, neurotic, and stressful world can be difficult. Not only have most of our instincts become dormant, but we rarely trust them. Your intuition or gut feeling can be a source of wisdom and, often, your best guide. But to receive this guidance, you have to listen to it and learn to understand what it's trying to tell you. This starts when you tune in to your inner self.

Your inner voice is nothing more than your subconscious telling you what's best for you under the circumstances. However, it may not say what you'd like to hear, and that's often the main reason why you choose to ignore this voice.

2. Develop emotional intelligence

Emotionally intelligent people have great people skills. They are not only in touch with their feelings, but are able to tune in to the feelings of others.

Emotional intelligence enables people to understand themselves and learn where their feelings are coming from. As a result, their reactions are timely and appropriate. They are good at listening, which not only improves their communication skills, but prevents emotionally-charged situations from getting out of hand.

Basically, managing emotions is about working out what triggered a particular emotion and not responding until you've had time to process that emotion. The best thing is that when you can manage your emotions, you can easily manage any situation you find yourself in.

3. Develop a positive mindset

Being positive about life is good for your health, your relations, and your overall happiness.

In line with the saying that "like attracts like," staying positive even when things are not going well is the prerequisite for success. When you are positive about life, it's easy to feel good about yourself, and this makes it easier to deal with anger—both yours and other people's.

4. **Mindfulness**

Applying mindfulness techniques is very useful when you feel you're beginning to lose it or feel you need more balance in your life. First of all, recognize what's happening (I'm getting angry). Give yourself time to think about how to respond (Count to ten). Respond calmly (Suggest a short break, postpone the meeting for another time, or try to look at the problem from a different angle or in a way that would give both parties a chance to reconsider their position).

5. **Identify your anger threshold**

You have to know when to draw the line and remove yourself from a situation that is not going anywhere and is likely to get out of hand. Depending on the situation, you may suggest a different approach, consult with someone, or simply walk away. Sometimes, removing yourself from the scene is all it takes to defuse a tense moment. However, it's important you do this BEFORE things get out of hand.

6. Recharge before start running on empty

Negative emotions, such as anger, create negative energy which is not only self-destructive, but quickly depletes your vitality and enthusiasm. To fight back, find out what activities boost your mood and do them whenever you feel subconscious negativity creeping up (this could be taking your dog for a walk, sitting in the garden, meditating, chatting to someone, listening to uplifting music, and so on).

To quote Zen Buddhist monk Thich Nhat Hanh, "When you say something unkind, when you do something in retaliation, your anger increases. You make the other person suffer, and they try hard to say or do something back to make you suffer, and get relief from their suffering. That is how conflict escalates."

Day 13

Emotional Intelligence and Anger Management

When most people think of emotional intelligence, they seem to imagine it as a set of skills that can make them more employable. This is partly true—being a good team player, working easily under pressure, and being able to communicate effectively in a culturally-diverse environment increases your chances of getting hired.

However, these same skills are just as important outside work, and maybe even more so. Your ability to understand and manage your emotions and be able to process them before responding will impact how successfully you deal with challenges on both the personal and professional level.

Emotional intelligence is much more than empathy and good people skills. It's about self-awareness and self-management: the very skills you need if you're struggling with anger.

What's Emotional Intelligence and Why Is It Important

Emotional intelligence skills revolve around the ability to understand and manage your own emotions, as well as those of others. Managing emotions is about understanding what triggers them, but choosing not to respond to the trigger until you've had time to process the emotion. And when you can manage your emotions, you can manage any situation you may find yourself in.

The ability to manage your emotions can be of great help in many different situations, like with decision-making or conflict resolution, but particularly with avoiding situations which could lead to conflict.

For anyone who has contact with others (as most of us do), conflicts are an unavoidable part of life. They are not necessarily bad, because they sometimes help get issues and emotions out in the open. So, if you can control your emotions, you can take control of your life and relationships.

Relationship problems happen both inside and outside of work, and although you would use a different technique when resolving a diplomatic conflict than an argument with a friend, you still need to be emotionally intelligent to successfully address the situation.

Learning about emotional intelligence is not difficult, though it comes easier to some than to others. For people who are empathic by nature, these skills are a way of life, and they— often unknowingly—apply them to whatever they do. On the other hand, those who are not in touch with their own feelings, and who care even less for the feelings of others, have to make an effort to start thinking and behaving in an emotionally intelligent way.

Many people learn emotional intelligence on the job, like when they find themselves in situations that require tolerance, patience, and empathy. However, it's much better to acquire these skills before you find yourself in a delicate situation.

What distinguishes emotionally intelligent people from others is that they know themselves well, so they understand why they think and react the way they do. When you have a high level of self-awareness, you understand what's going on in your mind, even if you don't approve of it. And it's easier to deal with something you understand.

We all get angry from time to time, but an emotionally intelligent person will always try to process the emotion they are experiencing. This is important, since your anger is often just a reaction to something else, even something you may not even be aware of like the memory of an old hurt.

Emotional competency can truly change your life and enhance your chances of success on all levels. There are many techniques at your disposal if you want to master emotional intelligence skills, but to truly benefit from them, you have to apply them to everything you do.

Emotional intelligence is also about developing an awareness of how your behavior affects others—an emotionally intelligent person is fully aware of this, regardless of the situation they find themselves in.

2 main benefits of emotional intelligence:

- **You're in complete control of your emotions**

When you can control your emotions, you can control your life. And when you can do that, you can take a proactive role in how your life pans out.

- **You easily avoid or resolve conflicts**

  Although emotionally intelligent people are good at resolving conflicts, their main advantage over others is that they know how to prevent a situation from getting to a stage where it becomes an open conflict.

How Emotional Intelligence Helps with Anger Management

Emotional intelligence is mainly about self-awareness and self-management. People who are self-aware rarely allow themselves to get carried away, even when feeling angry, while self-management helps them control their angry thoughts and emotions.

So, if you are often overwhelmed with negative thoughts, which create negative emotions and result in angry outbursts, you need to address your anger problem as soon as possible.

However, if you believe that your behavior does not require therapy, you can try and modify it by improving your emotional intelligence skills. This is only possible if you practice self-awareness, which can be achieved when you start paying attention to and trying to understand your thoughts, emotions, and behavior.

6 ways to develop emotional intelligence:

1. **Self-Analysis**

   If you really know yourself, you will understand why you feel and react the way you do. When you understand the WHY (you react a certain way), it becomes easier to figure out the HOW (you should behave instead).

2. **Self-awareness**

   Learn how to tune in to your emotions, regardless of what they are, and try to understand how they affect your thoughts or decisions. Ask yourself why you feel the way you do.

3. **Understand where your anger is coming from**

   Negative feelings are easier to deal with if you name them. Even if you can't do anything about them at the moment, knowing what you're dealing with is part of the solution.

4. **Don't rush to respond to a trigger**

   Whenever you feel angry, give yourself time to think before responding. Depending on what you're responding to, you may consider putting off your response for later. If that's not possible, simply count to 10, or 50, or as long it takes so you don't say something you may later regret.

5. **Try to tune in to the emotions of others**

Unfortunately, most people are neither good listeners nor do they have time to spare for others. Try approaching others with an open mind so you can "read" into the situation and get a feeling for how they feel.

6. **Be flexible**

Accept that regardless of how strong your views on a particular topic might be, there may be situations where you have to be more diplomatic. Be prepared to adjust your words, actions, or reactions to the situation.

7. **Recognize and name**

All emotions—especially negative ones—have to be recognized and named so you can address the REAL cause of your reaction.

8. **Emotional regulation**

This is about learning how to control your strong emotions, particularly negative ones, and not acting on impulse. Practice by thinking of something that will make you feel hurt, angry, or exploited. Sit with the feeling—feel it, "digest" it—and after about five minutes, "respond" to the person or situation that made you feel that way.

You can't manage a situation (or a team, a relationship, etc.) unless you can manage yourself. We live under a lot of stress, which often makes otherwise peaceful people lash out in anger. Although shouting, slamming doors, or using strong language can help you release that pent-up anger, such behavior is unacceptable in public. The benefits of getting rid of your anger will be weakened by the fact that you'll later have to apologize to those who felt hurt or threatened by your behavior. And it may even cost you your job, or a relationship.

The key advantage of being emotionally intelligent is that you become more aware of how what you say and do affects those around you. It not only makes you a better leader, but also a better human being.

Day 14

Emotional Intelligence

In the overpopulated, dynamic, and fast-changing world, it's becoming difficult to cope—let alone succeed personally and professionally—without emotional intelligence skills. However, the dwindling job market, overcrowded workspaces, and increasing demands on our time all contribute to the stress and frustration we have to deal with almost on a daily basis.

Managing one's emotions is key to emotional intelligence, but this doesn't mean you have to feel positive about life regardless of what's going on around you.

Managing your emotions is about learning to react to fear, frustration, disappointment, or stress in a way that will reduce anxiety and tension in both yourself and others, rather than make an already tense situation worse.

Recognizing and Managing Your Emotions

Our emotions are the result of our thoughts, experiences, and mindset. And although it's not possible to change your past experiences, it is possible to change your thoughts and your attitude.

You may be feeding yourself negative thoughts, or you may be in a situation where you are fed such thoughts by those around you, such as your parents, partner, or friends.

Fortunately, thoughts can be changed and the power to change your thoughts and behavior lies with you.

It's unrealistic to expect anyone, no matter how emotionally intelligent they are, to always feel positive about life. Much of how we feel and think has to do with the people we come into contact with or the environments we live in. For example, in a war zone or a poverty-stricken neighborhood, it's difficult to be positive about anything, especially if you feel stuck. Many people feel just bad about themselves or their lives despite having everything they could wish for.

To manage emotions, you must never suppress them. This is why many therapists disapprove of mantras and positive affirmations. Instead of acknowledging you are sick, without an income, or in a messy relationship, by repeating a positive mantra—"I'll be fine", or "I am healthy and full of energy" or "I am confident the Universe will provide"—you are wasting time waiting for someone else to provide a solution to your problem.

Positive affirmations can be very helpful when you're feeling down, because it's definitely better to believe your circumstances will improve than it is to tell yourself you're in a hopeless situation. However, this only works as a temporary measure, until you find a creative solution to your problem. In other words, positive affirmations are simply a tool for boosting your self-confidence until you actually do something about the problem. The focus is on action.

There may be occasions when pushing your emotions out of your mind may help you deal with them. When powerful feelings stay bottled up for too long, especially if they concern a traumatic experience, they can affect your behavior, health, and mindset.

Managing emotions is not about repressing them, but addressing them in a positive and constructive way.

3 tips on how to prevent negative emotions from becoming bottled up:

1. **Talk about them**

   Emotions become bottled up because some experiences are not easy to talk about, you may not know how to express your feelings, or you may have no one to talk to. Some people may also think expressing emotions is a sign of weakness.

   An emotionally intelligent person knows that releasing emotions is an important part of mental health, necessary for your emotional and mental well-being.

   Unaddressed emotions eventually become emotional baggage, which some people carry around their whole life. Your emotional health depends on your memories and experiences, and the more traumas in your life, the greater the need to unpack that emotional baggage and let it go. On their own, old wounds may heal on the surface, but memories of shame, grief, guilt, or regret can create scars which, if unreleased, may stay with you forever.

2. **Write them down**

   If you can't talk about your emotions, try writing them
   down. That way, you can still get them out of your
   system without anyone learning about your secret. To
   make sure no one sees, destroy the written evidence
   once you've finished.

3. **Learn how to get rid of negative emotions**

   There are many ways to let go of anger, fear, sadness,
   jealousy, and other negative emotions. If these
   emotions are so overwhelming they are preventing
   you from leading a normal life, you should consider
   therapy. If they are less problematic, you can try self-
   help techniques, like physical exercise, journaling,
   self-therapy, meditation. Getting rid of negative
   emotions is particularly important if you have low
   self-esteem and a tendency to turn your anger inward.

However, try as you may, some types of anger may not be
possible to get rid of. Either because the injustice done is
unforgivable, like child abuse, or because you simply can't
get over something, such as someone much less competent
than you being promoted and becoming your boss.

However, although anger may be justified, holding on to it is
not. If the damage cannot be undone, for your own peace of
mind, you should try to resolve the negative effect of anger.
This is crucial because as long as you're holding on to it, it
will continue to harm you—without you even realizing it.

The Burden of Unresolved Anger

We often, unknowingly, hold on to anger by revisiting painful memories from the past which we can't or won't let go.

To let go of the anger, you first have to understand how self-destructive it can be and how it can cause many problems without you even realizing what's going on.

All emotions need an outlet. When anger is not released, it affects your body, which affects how your mind works, which in turn affects what sort of emotions you end up living with. Instead of letting repressed anger rule your life, take charge by letting go of everything that is no longer serving you, or that is undermining your health and well-being.

4 steps to letting go of anger:

Step 1: Are you aware of how anger is affecting your life?

To see the full impact of how anger is making you feel and behave, write down the answers to these questions.

1. How does anger make you feel?
2. How much time each day do you spend feeling angry?
3. Do you often wake up feeling angry?
4. Is anger often preventing you from falling asleep?
5. Do you indulge in comfort foods or alcohol when feeling angry? Does it help?
6. How does anger affect your performance at work?

7. How does anger affect your personal relationships?

8. What would it take for you to let go of this anger?

Step 2: Imagine your life without this bottled-up anger

Write down your answers.

1. If you didn't feel angry, how would you feel in the morning upon waking up?

2. If you didn't feel angry, would you drink less?

3. How would not feeling angry affect your relationships?

4. How would not feeling angry affect your performance at work?

5. How would you feel about your future if you didn't have this anger?

Step 3: Accept the things you cannot change

Have you identified the real cause of your anger? If you could turn back time, what would you do differently that would make it possible to live free of anger?

1. List three things you would change in your behavior.

2. What's stopping you from changing those behaviors now?

3. Can you accept your regrets as mistakes you can learn from?

Step 4: Acceptance

Think about your anger. Write down your answers.

1. Are you in any way responsible for the hurt that's making you angry?

2. Have you considered the possibility that the person who made you angry had no other option?

3. Have YOU ever done something similar to someone else?

Step four can be painful but is very powerful. Depending on the source of your anger, it may take you a long time to get to a stage where you can look at the problem from the other person's point of view.

It's believed that only once you take full responsibility for your anger, and understand your own role in it, can you truly get over it.

Day 15

Mindfulness

Mindfulness is about being fully focused on what's going on around you, what you're doing, what you're saying, and how you're feeling. Although this probably sounds simple enough, it's easier said than done—our minds are not easy to keep still.

Due to stress, information overload, or busy lifestyle, keeping your mind from wandering can be quite a challenge. The racing thoughts, the inner chatter, or things you unconsciously worry about all the time, can make your mind cluttered and restless.

The key to mindful living is the focus. A mindful person is totally in the moment, whether he's playing with his child, working, eating, making love, rock climbing, or writing a letter to a friend. He's aware of the effect his words or actions may have on others, so he thinks before he speaks or acts.

Mindfulness can be learned and it can also become a way of life; however, it does require an effort on your part to keep your mind focused on one thing amidst all the distractions that surround us. Many activities can help you cultivate this personal development technique, such as yoga, meditation, visualization, and sports.

How Mindful Are You?

Practicing mindfulness has many benefits for your health, happiness, work, and relationships. Both science and experience show all areas of your life improve once you start living mindfully.

However, being mindful in this day and age is not easy. Studies indicate most people spend nearly 50% of their waking hours thinking about something that has nothing to do with what they are doing, and this indirectly affects their performance, creativity, concentration, and well-being.

13 things a MINDFUL person does:

1. They find it easy to focus on tasks.

2. They make good use of their time.

3. They get things done promptly.

4. They are not easily distracted.

5. They prioritize and stay focused on the most important things.

6. They always find time to respond to emails, meet friends, and visit family.

7. They are fully present during meetings.

8. They find it easy to concentrate on what they're doing.

9. They think before saying something.

10. They choose to "sleep on it" rather than make a hasty decision.

11. They stay calm under pressure.

12. They are fully aware of how they feel about someone or something.

13. They find it easy to understand how others feel.

8 things THOSE WHO LACK mindfulness do:

1. They are often surprised by what they say or do.

2. They often multitask.

3. They worry about work even after leaving office.

4. They often forget things other people say, things they read about, or promises   they make.

5. They are uncomfortable sitting still or being quiet for long, and would rather be   doing something.

6. Their mind wanders.

7. When they are upset, they can't stop thinking about it.

8. They often have trouble sleeping because their thoughts keep them awake.

Our scattered minds do the best they can to keep track of all the things we need to remember. However, in this stressful world, we wear so many hats in a single day that it's small wonder we are often highly-strung and anxious.

3 simple mindfulness exercises that will force you to slow down and focus on something:

1. Mindful observation

This exercise will help you notice, perhaps for the first time, how beautiful, unusual, or interesting some things you never thought about before are.

Choose an object from your immediate environment, like your garden, the park you walk your dog in, or something you keep on your balcony. It should be something that's been there for years, which you never bothered to notice before—a flower, a bird that visits your bird feeder, a piece of rock, a fallen tree trunk, a tree in full blossom.

Look at the object for as long as you can stay focused. Relax as you do so.

Examine its shape, color, and size, picking up even the tiniest details. As you do so, try to tune in to this object and imagine what its purpose in the web of life must be.

If you can get yourself to stay focused for 15 minutes without answering your phone or talking to someone, you'll be amazed at how refreshed you'll feel afterward.

2. Mindful immersion

This exercise is about finding contentment in what you do instead of moving continually from one activity to another. The purpose is to enjoy whatever it is you are doing at the moment.

For example, if you are involved in otherwise boring and repetitive work, such as doing housework, working in the garden, or sorting out files at work, try to approach these tasks from a different angle. Make your work more creative.

Pay attention to every single detail of your activity, as if you had to describe to someone how such a job should be done. Focus on what you are doing, and focus on how your body feels, how your muscles move as you lift or move things around.

By becoming aware of every step and immersing yourself in it, the job will be finished quickly. You'll stop thinking how boring it is and you'll stop pushing yourself to get it over with as soon as possible so you can move on to something else. You may even start enjoying it.

3. Mindful loving

When you are mindful in love, you don't wait for someone's birthday, anniversary, or Valentine's day to reflect on the importance of that relationship in your life. From time to time, stop and look back on the connection you have with a friend, spouse, or a parent. Reflect on all you've been through, appreciate that they are in your life, and show them you care. Don't just *think* about how much they mean to you—tell them how you feel.

Mindfulness and Anger Management

Cultivating mindfulness helps you reduce both the frequency and the level of the anger you experience.

Mindfulness is about being fully present in whatever you do. To some, this comes naturally, but most of us have to learn how to cultivate mindfulness. And one of the easiest ways to learn this is through meditation.

The practice of mindfulness meditation does not have to be complicated. You can do it while walking your dog, sitting quietly in the garden, listening to uplifting music, or as a part of other activities such as yoga, sports, or knitting. Simply put, mindfulness is about being "centered," without being aware of it. With practice, it becomes a way of life.

Mindfulness can make it easier to cope with life while improving your physical health by relieving stress, lowering blood pressure, and reducing chronic pain.

If your life decisions are made mindfully, it means you will have thought them through. For example, if you decide to go vegan, a mindful approach to this decision should be well thought-through and creative.

5 characteristics of mindful vegans:

- They understand and accept the challenges that a new way of life brings.
- They are prepared to leave their comfort zone and give up the things they are used to, in order to allow new tastes, experiences, and people into their lives.
- They have a strategy on how to deal with crisis, cravings, or self-doubts.

- They are not afraid to stand up for what they believe in and are prepared to explain, but also defend, their way of life without confrontation.
- They prepare and eat their food mindfully.

So, how do you apply mindfulness to anger management?

While some therapists recommend controlling anger—by counting to 10, or by hitting a pillow—others disagree with this approach as they believe this only heals the wound on the surface, while deep inside, it continues to fester. Instead, they recommend addressing the real problem behind the angry outburst, not the anger itself.

Regardless of their approach to anger management, more and more therapists recommend replacing traditional anger management techniques with mindfulness techniques.

Mindfulness is a very personal experience and there are many different ways of doing it, but, you can apply these steps to almost any activity or any situation.

7 basic steps to mindfulness:

1. Find a quiet spot to sit down and relax.

2. Set a time limit, like five to 10 minutes.

3. Still your mind and if it wanders, bring it back.

4. Become aware of your body: notice how your knees feel, how warm or cold your feet are, how tense or relaxed your abdomen is, or if you have any pains or aches.

5. Become aware of the noises around you: try to guess which bird is making that particular noise, what's going on in the street, whose dog is barking.

6. Become aware of any unusual smells: a neighbor having a barbecue, your roommate making a cup of coffee, the scent of lilac in the garden.

7. Slowly come back.

Day 16

Meditation

Numerous studies confirm that meditating for just 20 minutes a day, every day, can have numerous positive effects on both physical and mental health. This is largely because meditation relaxes the mind, which in turn reduces anger and anxiety, lowers blood pressure, and helps you feel grounded.

For those who practice it regularly, meditation can become a way of life. It can also help you come face to face with the feelings you keep hidden from others—or yourself. In the case of those who've suffered trauma or some kind of emotional or physical abuse, meditation can bring healing from the pain, shame, or guilt that is often present. This type of healing is particularly effective if you carry a lot of old, repressed anger.

Meditation is a skill, which means it can be taught and perfected with practice. There are many different ways to do it, and you can choose the style that suits you most based on what you want to achieve with it (e.g., calming vs. insight meditation), or which tradition, culture, or spiritual discipline you want to follow.

Of the dozens of types of meditation practiced today, the most popular ones are guided or unguided meditation, walking meditation, Buddhist meditation, Transcendental meditation, and meditation for sleep, for stress, for anger, for compassion.

The point is, there is no right or wrong way to meditate. Meditation is a very personal experience, and you should choose the one that works for you.

Where to Meditate

Meditation does not have to be a complicated affair, with a special practice space, dimmed lights, and uplifting music. Ideally, it should be practiced in a space dedicated to that purpose, however, that is optional.

Some people go to great lengths to create special effects in the meditation room, but these help only in the sense that they create an atmosphere in which it becomes easier to switch off and relax, and are in no way essential for successful meditation. With practice, you can learn to slip into a meditative state anywhere, regardless of the external and internal "noise."

3 things to bear in mind when creating a meditation space at home:

- **Find a space**

    Very few of us can set aside an entire room for meditation, so meditation space is usually a corner of a room which has another purpose, like a bedroom or a study. The meditation space can also be a table decorated for that purpose, a bookshelf, or even a tree trunk or a bench in the garden.

- **Decorate the space**

  This is what will make it conducive to meditation. As meditation is a very personal experience, anything that helps you enter a meditative state is fine—a statue of Buddha, unusual pieces of rock or wood, crystals, candles, photographs, flowers, dry leaves, fruits.

- **Make your space sacred, i.e. special**

  You make your meditation space sacred by making it look and "feel" special compared to other parts of your living space. This is why you should never keep "mundane" things in it, like books, magazines, food, or clothes.

Health Benefits of Meditation

While, for most people, meditation is a relaxation process, in Ayurveda, it's a detoxifying one—it helps clear "waste" products from the mind. It revolves around training your mind to focus and release negative mental energy that affects your thoughts, emotions, and behavior.

Meditation affects all aspects of our being:

- On an emotional level, it's an effective tool for beating stress, depression, and anxiety.

- On a mental level, it helps still your inner chatter so you can concentrate and relax more easily while ignoring distracting thoughts.

- On a physical level, it calms you down. When your heartbeat slows and blood pressure drops, your brain produces alpha, instead of beta waves. After spending some time in this relaxed but alert alpha state, you'll feel as refreshed as if you've had a nap.

Numerous studies show that regular meditators are generally healthier than non-meditators, and that meditation helps not only with stress-related disorders but with many other modern-day diseases like migraines, irritable bowel syndrome, asthma, anxiety, mild depression, high blood pressure, and heart disease.

Meditation techniques

Meditation is about stilling your mind and emptying it of distracting thoughts. It's best if you can meditate at the same time and place every day. How long you do it for is unimportant, as long as you do it properly. If you are new to meditation, start with 10 minutes a day, and by the end of the week, you should start to notice improvements.

Basic meditation technique:

1. Sit comfortably—either in the lotus position or, if your back is weak, in a straight-backed chair with your feet on the floor.

2. Close your eyes. Calm down.

3. Breathe slowly and steadily.

4. To keep yourself focused, you can repeat a mantra and gaze at a *mandala* or a candle flame. This is optional.

5. When you have finished, slowly open your eyes, move your arms and legs to encourage circulation, then stand up. Have a glass of water to ground yourself, as some people feel dizzy after sitting still for a long time.

Types of Meditation

The type of meditation you choose to do should be the one that works for you and should address the reason you are doing it—to calm down, to gain spiritual insight, to sleep better, and so on.

Meditation for stress and anxiety

Life is stressful as is, but if your day starts with traffic-induced stress and ends the same way—especially if you spend long hours getting to and from work—this can quickly become too much.

The reason consistent, daily meditation is so effective for stress-management is that it helps you reprogram your brain so it becomes less reactive and more responsive.

Stress usually makes people worry too much, and the racing thoughts make it difficult to focus on anything. Meditation is a very useful tool to quiet an overactive mind. With regular practice, you can learn how to detach yourself from the endless thoughts—not by forgetting about them, but by controlling how much you stay with them.

Meditation for anger

While there are different forms of meditation to choose from, the so-called "anger meditation" is aimed at addressing your anger problem not by controlling your anger, but by letting it run its course.

To this effect, meditation helps shift your focus from thinking about who or what made you angry to the actual feeling of anger. Feel the rage, embarrassment, frustration, or whatever other emotions your anger provokes. If there is a part of your body that is hot or burning with anger, like your face, stomach, or head, become aware of it.

Focus on that spot, and start breathing slowly and deeply. Try to bring your breath to that area. Keep going until you can feel the negative energy dissolve.

Meditation for sleep

This type of meditation teaches you not to get caught up in negative thoughts before going to bed. For many people, it isn't until they go to bed, or just before they do so, that they can finally slow down and relax. It is then that they start mulling over the day behind them or ahead of them. So, instead of getting themselves ready sleep by slowing down, they activate their mind by thinking about the various problems they have to deal with or the tasks awaiting them in the morning.

Meditation for sleep is usually a guided meditation that will help you let go of whatever you are thinking about until you become relaxed enough to fall asleep. This process revolves around the fact that meditation helps lower the heart rate and encourages slower breathing.

To help fight insomnia, don't think, read, or watch anything exciting that could start you thinking or worrying. Instead, focus on something calming and peaceful, like a photo, music, or thought, and watch your body wind down as it prepares for sleep.

Guided vs. unguided meditation

In guided meditation, you are led through meditation "moves" by a teacher who takes you through all the steps of a particular meditation technique and who suggests how you can apply what you've learned into your everyday life. This type of meditation is particularly good for beginners.

During unguided or silent meditation, you meditate on your own, either completely alone or as part of a group, and no one explains the process. This can be as simple as sitting quietly and concentrating on your breath while emptying your mind of distracting thoughts, or you can apply a particular meditation technique (like meditation for anger, sleep, and so on).

Zen meditation

Zen meditation focuses on breath and how it moves through your body. You think of nothing and let the mind "just be."

With this type of meditation, you cultivate both mindfulness and alertness.

Mantra meditation

With this type of meditation, instead of focusing on the breath to quiet the mind, you focus on a mantra. Your mantra could consist of a syllable, word, or a phrase which sums up what you believe in or what you aspire to.

The philosophy behind the mantra meditation is that the subtle vibrations associated with the repeated mantra can encourage positive change, boost self-confidence, reduce fear, and encourage empathy. Basically, a mantra should guide you in the way you want to live your life, so you choose a mantra that strikes a chord with you.

You can choose a quote:

- "Our greatest glory is not in never falling, but in rising every time we fall." (Confucius)
- "A person is what he or she thinks about all day long." (Ralph Waldo Emerson)
- "Opportunities don't happen, you create them." (Chris Groser)
- "They cannot take away your self-respect if you don't give it to them." (Mahatma Gandhi)

You can also create a personal mantra which sums up your goals and aspirations:

- I can and I will
- Live simply
- I write my destiny
- Seize the day

Transcendental meditation (TM)

TM is a silent mantra meditation, usually practiced for 20 minutes twice a day, although there are many variations. You meditate with your eyes closed and repeat a mantra assigned to you by your teacher. While you meditate this way, your thinking process "transcends" and is replaced by a state of pure consciousness.

Unlike other types of meditation, TM requires formal training by a certified teacher. It does not require concentration or contemplation, just breathing normally and focusing your attention on the mantra.

Some studies suggest that this type of meditation is not a good choice for those suffering from a certain psychiatric condition.

Walking meditation

During walking meditation, you are physically active and focused on the experience of walking. You walk very slowly and concentrate on your breath. Ideally, you should do this in a place where you will not be distracted by either people, traffic, or scenery.

You can practice barefoot or wear light shoes, and you can walk in a circle if you are doing this in a small garden. Try to be aware of the sounds around you and of yourself moving in that particular location. Walking meditation is a great technique for improving concentration.

The internationally-renowned self-help author and motivational speaker Wayne Dyer had great advice how life should be lived: "Become slower in your journey through life. Practice yoga and meditation if you suffer from 'hurry sickness.' Become more introspective by visiting quiet places such as churches, museums, mountains, and lakes. Give yourself permission to read at least one novel a month for pleasure."

Day 17

Zen Buddhism and the Importance of Living in the Present

What is perhaps the most striking difference between Zen Buddhism and Western culture is the understanding of happiness. While most people would define happiness as getting what they want—having a certain way of life or certain material possessions—Zen philosophy is based on the idea that we should stop expecting our lives to develop the way we think they should.

Unfortunately, the more we look for something to make us happy, the more likely we are to be disappointed. But for Buddhists, true happiness is a state of mind, and they look deep within when searching for it.

Zen tools that can help you reach a stage when you start looking for fulfillment within, rather than without, are meditation, mindfulness, and the practice of loving kindness.

Living according to these principles not only makes it easier to find your bliss, but makes it very difficult to develop any negative emotions—particularly anger.

What is Zen About?

While interest in Zen Buddhism is growing, many believe that following this philosophy is not possible in the 21st century. It's true that the modern world is very different from the time when Buddhism first appeared; however, the main obstacle to a Zen way of life is that obsession with material possessions, consumerism, and personal ambition—not spiritual development—have become the core values of Western culture.

Zen is about peaceful simplicity, but the stress of everyday life makes it difficult to aim for harmony within. Still, it's possible to embrace Zen values if you manage to slow down and live mindfully.

5 steps to adopting Zen philosophy amidst the chaos of modern life:

1. Find your meditation technique

Meditation is key for the Zen way of life, so choose how you want to do it. There are many styles to choose from, but the most important element of successful meditation is being focused. If you have a busy lifestyle and multitasking helps you cope, be prepared to give up that way of life. Your overall performance and results in anything you do will improve greatly if you start concentrating on one thing at a time.

2. Enjoy the moment

Learn to be content with who you are and what you have. When you learn to accept the life you are living, you stop worrying, and when you are free of worry you enjoy life more. Savoring every moment amidst the stress and chaos we're drowning in is not easy, but it's the only way to keep life from passing you by.

The well-known Vietnamese Zen Monk Thich Nhat Hanh said it all: "Drink your tea slowly and reverently, as if it is the axis on which the world earth revolves slowly, evenly, without rushing toward the future."

3. Look for happiness within

Some people are happy wherever they are, while others are unhappy, regardless. It's pointless to look for happiness in far-off places, better-paid jobs, or faster cars. Happiness is wherever you are right now, because it is within you. Instead of searching for it far and wide, look deep within.

4. Do one thing at a time

Most people have to juggle family, career, and social life, so multitasking has become a way of life. However, when you live like this, all you are doing is shifting your focus from one thing to another throughout the day. When you are not fully focused, and instead trying to do several things at the same time, a lot of your energy and time is wasted. You achieve much more if you give your full attention to whatever you're doing, rather than hoping to get more things done by taking on multiple tasks.

5. Be kind to yourself and others

In some ways, Buddhism and emotional intelligence are based on the same values: understanding, empathy, and forgiveness. When you learn to forgive (both yourself and others), you stop judging and blaming. When you try to understand why someone has done something that upset you, you stop feeling angry. When you practice gratitude, you realize how good life actually is. Whatever you decide to do, don't underestimate the power of kindness.

Zen Approach to Anger

We all get angry from time to time, but we deal with this powerful emotion in different ways. Some cultures repress it, while others express it freely—some even enjoy the feeling.

From the Zen point of view, feeling angry is simply wasting your energy on a mental state which serves no purpose. Buddhists approach anger in a pragmatic way—while they don't deny it, they will do nothing to help it grow.

While psychologists tell us anger is normal and we should express it in a constructive way, in Buddhism, anger is seen as the most negative and destructive force—one which can easily destroy all the good in the world. So, they approach anger in a typically Buddhist way: by neutralizing it with non-anger.

<u>5 Zen things to do when you start getting angry:</u>

1. It's OK to be angry, don't deny it

To Buddhists, fear and anger are energy-draining emotions which can control your life if you let them. With patience and practice, you can learn to avoid these mental states.

2. Learn how not to get angry

In Buddhism, anger gets a bad reputation—mainly because it revolves around ego. Still, Buddhists believe in practicing loving kindness even with those who make them angry. Buddhists don't behave aggressively when angry, nor do they try to suppress anger. They deal with it by observing it, but not participating in it. In other words, they neutralize it with understanding and compassion.

3. Cultivate patience

If you can't help feeling angry, give yourself time to calm down so you can communicate without making a scene or causing harm. Acknowledge the anger and embrace it. Wait. Given enough time, and your anger will vanish on its own. Patience gives you the chance to analyze your angry feelings and understand why you feel a certain way.

4. Don't feed anger

While some therapists recommend venting your anger in a way that will not cause harm, like pounding on a pillow, Buddhists believe that when you express your anger, either verbally or physically, you help it grow. When you ignore it, though, you starve it.

5. Compassion takes courage

Many people feel strong when they are angry, probably because of the adrenaline rush that floods the brain, and regard those who never show anger as weak cowards. In Buddhism, it's the other way around.

Buddhists believe showing anger is a sign of weakness, while having the strength to acknowledge anger, or the fear you feel when facing an angry person or when in a dangerous situation, is a sign of real strength.

Like most Eastern philosophies, Zen Buddhism teachings focus on acceptance and patience. Zen teaches us to be observant of what's going on around us and to embrace both the good and the bad, for there is a reason for everything.

As Robert Green pointed out, "Everything that happens to you is a form of instruction if you pay attention."

Day 18

Inner Peace Techniques for Anger Management

None of us go through life unscathed and, over time, we all devise various coping strategies to help us deal with stress, problems, anger, and disappointments. However, not all coping strategies are healthy.

The unhealthy coping strategies are what most people typically fall back on, mainly because these require the least effort and offer instant gratification. Unfortunately, they often have long-term negative effects on our health. These strategies include alcohol, drugs, antidepressants, smoking, and comfort eating.

On the other hand, healthy coping strategies, which offer a better long-term solution, are not always easy to implement and it may take quite some time for the first improvements to show.

Healthy anger management strategies are based on techniques which help you take control of your emotions and minimize the effects of angry outbursts. Eastern philosophies, such as Buddhism, Taoism, and Yoga, recommend gentle, yet powerful and effective, ways of managing anger that focus on inner peace and self-discipline.

The Tao of Inner Peace

Taoism is a belief system that promotes self-acceptance, inner peace, and flexibility. The reason Taoism and other Eastern philosophies have become so popular in the West is that as life becomes more complex and people find themselves facing overwhelming challenges on all levels, they try to find an alternative way of dealing with stress and restoring inner balance.

Taoism teaches many things, the most important of which is that the past is behind you and the future is not here yet— you should focus on the present moment. And this is why these ideas are so difficult for many to grasp. In the West, people spend their entire lives ruminating about their past mistakes and worrying about how they'll cope with the future. Being overwhelmed by uncertainty (because they constantly worry about the future) and mentally exhausted (from constantly thinking about what happened in the past) are the main reasons why anxiety, depression, and mental disorders are rising to epidemic proportions in the developed world.

Tao is big on forgiveness, so its approach to anger management is to forgive. Whether or not you forgive doesn't really matter, however, as it won't change what happened in the past. Which leads us to Taoism's key take on life— acceptance. Accept the past for what it is, because it's been and gone. Focus on the here and now.

Taoism is not a religion, but a belief system whose main doctrine is that only harmony within people can create harmony in the environment. It deals with anger by cultivating empathy, even for those who make practitioners angry. Through the constant search for inner peace, Taoists develop the ability to understand the suffering of others—even their enemies—without judgment.

<u>4 Taoist tips on achieving inner peace:</u>

Find your own happiness

People need different things to feel fulfilled. There is no recipe to finding happiness, because happiness means different things to different people. It's only when you find your own meaning in life that you will have found true happiness.

Peace is not around you—it's inside you

To reach a stage where you can find peace amidst crowds, noise, and chaos, you have to be able to switch off—regardless of what's going on around or inside you. This is achieved through meditation, which is a great tool for developing self-discipline.

Drop expectations

Expectations are a major cause of anger, because they make you over-ambitious, competitive, and frustrated. People are rarely satisfied with what they have and always want more. According to Taoism, the more you expect, the less you become: the key to happiness is to live in the present and practice gratitude.

Simplify your life

When you declutter your life and your mind from all the unnecessary things, thoughts, and information, you create space for the people and experiences that really matter.

Yoga

Despite the way many people approach yoga, it is much more than a workout. It's a spiritual tradition that brings together the body, mind, and spirit, and *asanas* are only a small part of it. According to yoga philosophy, the main purpose of physical exercises is to prepare the body for long periods of meditation, because you need to be mentally strong and physically flexible to be able to sit still for extended periods of time.

 inner balance. Its three main elements are *pranayama* (breathing exercises), meditation, and *asanas* (physical exercises). And this is where many people who do yoga get it wrong.

To most people (in the West, at least), yoga is merely a way of exercising their bodies. However, although these exercises have proven health benefits, that's not what yoga is really about. Without *pranayama*, ethical practices, and meditation, you are not really practicing yoga.

This means that if you can do only simple poses but understand and follow the philosophy of yoga, you are at a much higher level of yoga practice than someone who can do even the most demanding exercises without understanding why they are doing it.

There are many different schools of yoga, but they all revolve around balance in the mind and body. And, just like other spiritual traditions, yoga can teach us how to react to anger without repressing it or acting aggressively.

According to yoga philosophy, anger should be avoided at all costs because it undermines the very essence of yoga—achieving happiness and freedom.

The ancient yogis firmly believed in and practiced the mind-body approach to life. To them, anger was a kind of blockage at the mental, physical, or spiritual level. To free up the blocked energy, they used a combination of asanas, *pranayama*, and meditation techniques as main anger management tools with which they distracted the angry mind from the negative thoughts. The basic yoga model for controlling anger is to stop the inner chatter (with meditation) and shift the focus from the anger trigger to exercise and breathing (with *asanas* and *pranayama*).

These practices help with anger management by putting you in a mental state which promotes tranquility and boosts self-esteem while improving your physical health through balancing the production of hormones.

<u>3 ways yoga helps control your anger:</u>

1. **Yoga calms you down**

Meditation and breathing techniques are the essence of yoga. They help you stop the inner chatter—and once that happens, it's easier to feel relaxed and stress-free. Anyone who has attended a yoga class knows how light and calm they feel afterward. This is because yoga practice reduces stress hormones (cortisol and adrenaline) and induces the relaxation response (by raising levels of oxytocin, a hormone that reduces blood pressure and improves the levels of certain neurotransmitters that are usually low in those who are overwhelmed with negativity). And it is only in this relaxed state of mind that we can clearly "see" the real reason for our anger or anxiety and come to terms with it. So, there is science-based evidence that yoga practice starts a number of positive chemical changes within your body.

2. **Yoga boosts your confidence**

Doing yoga helps build your physical and mental strength, which in turn boosts how you feel about yourself and your body. As your body becomes more supple, your skin more radiant, and you begin to walk more gracefully, you can't but feel proud of yourself. Another reason your confidence soars is that yoga improves your health on both the physical and mental levels, which indirectly affects how you feel about yourself and your life.

3. **Yoga unblocks your energy**

Yoga is all about the balance of the body, mind, and soul. For this to happen, the energy within your body has to flow freely. Unfortunately, it is often blocked due to prolonged stress, chronic fatigue, repressed emotions, fear, or depression. As a result, emotions can become unbalanced, and you may easily become overwhelmed with negativity. When energy "flows" freely, so do your emotions, and healthy emotions produce healthy thoughts.

There are several asanas that are particularly powerful when used for the release of pent up anger and frustration, and *garbhasana* and *koormasana*are believed to be the most eficient ones.

According to the well-known yoga teacher and author, TKV Desikachar, "The success of yoga does not lie in the ability to perform postures but in how it positively changes the way we live our lives and our relationships."

Day 19

Cognitive Behavioral Therapy

Anger can have many triggers and, depending on one's temperament, culture, and level of emotional intelligence, can be a positive or a destructive force. We start learning about anger management from the moment we are born: babies cry with anger if they are left hungry or wet; some children throw tantrums if they can't get what they want, while others try to get the same thing by being nice and sweet; and as adults, we learn to deal with frustrations almost on a daily basis.

However, when we find ourselves in situations that are far too complex to be resolved on our own, or when faced with mental health disorders which require a professional approach, it's best to seek a good therapist.

Anger Management Counseling

Counseling works for many mental disorders, including anger management. While there are many different approaches to this problem, perhaps best-known is cognitive-behavioral therapy (CBT). The best thing about it is that you can achieve considerable improvements relatively quickly, in about two months.

CBT's approach to anger management is to address a combination of situations and beliefs which may have contributed to how you feel about yourself, as well as to the reasons when and why you experience anger. It focuses mainly on your childhood experiences and treatment, including the beliefs you were fed with and whether you were mistreated or belittled.

However, there are many other types of therapy, and the anger symptoms you are experiencing may help you decide which one would be the best for you.

3 types of anger symptoms:

1. **Physiological** (rapid heart rate, shaking, aggression towards others, etc.)

2. **Cognitive** (difficulties concentrating or remembering, dreaming of revenge, etc.)

3. **Behavioral** (arguments which result in violence, reckless driving, alcohol abuse, etc.)

People struggling with mental disorders often struggle to determine which therapy would work best for them. With so many options to choose from, it's perhaps best to consult your doctor for advice on this. Still, you should also familiarize yourself with what each therapy consists of, for there may be some that would suit you more.

Different anger management therapies:

- **In-person therapy**

  This is when you see a therapist on a regular basis

over an extended period of time. It can be over the phone or online, in a group or on a one-to-one basis.

- **Online counseling**

  This is a relatively new type of counseling and requires you to have a computer or a smartphone. For many, it offers an original and innovative method of treatment. Although this type of therapy would save you a lot of time, it may not suit those who prefer face-to-face interaction or lack IT skills.

- **Group therapy**

  The best thing about this kind of therapy is that it provides both a therapist and a support group. This type of counseling is often preferred by those who enjoy being part of a group and don't mind discussing their problems in front of other people. They also stand to benefit from listening to what sort of problems others may be facing and how they cope with them.

- **Residential anger management**

  This type of therapy is more intense and is used for people whose lives have been severely affected by their inability to deal with anger. On the upside, clients are away from their everyday life and can focus completely on the therapy, but this kind of treatment takes a lot of commitment, and not everyone is able to be away from their job or families for an extended period of time.

Another option is to treat anger management with medication, which usually involves antidepressants, mood stabilizers, or antipsychotic drugs.

Medication is prescribed to patients with severe anger problems, but usually only as a short-term solution until they have calmed down and can start therapy. Drugs are generally avoided, as they often come with side effects and there is the possibility of addiction. For this reason, medication is usually recommended only as a temporary solution.

Cognitive Behavioral Therapy (CBT)

Cognitive behavioral therapy (CBT), which is successfully used for many different disorders, is based on the idea that the best way to stop the vicious cycle of negative thoughts, emotions, and behavior is to replace the destructive thought patterns with positive ones.

CBT is very effective in anger management and focuses on teaching patients both how to control their thoughts and emotions and how to interpret them in a positive way.

7 steps of anger management with CBT:

1. **Avoid negative thoughts**

Those who are always negative about life will never be able to see anything positive around them. If your mind is overwhelmed with negativity, you need to learn to look at life from a different angle and realize that things are not as bad as you may have thought.

CBT is about looking at the world, and your life, with more objectivity, and realizing how much your negative thoughts "color" your experiences. When you learn to change the way you react to situations which provoke negative emotions, you will know that your anger management therapy has succeeded. For example, stop feeling that jokes about overweight people are always aimed at you, stop beating yourself up for not having done more for your grandparents while they were alive, or focus on improving your performance instead of worrying you might lose your job.

Your thoughts affect your feelings, and vice versa—a negative thought pattern eventually turns to anger or self-anger. You don't have to have happy thoughts all the time, but neither should you focus only on thoughts which make you fearful, anxious, or angry. It's not a cliché that a positive state of mind creates opportunities and attracts positive experiences.

2. **Identify where your anger is coming from**

The main aim of CBT therapy is to get patients to understand what initiates the cycle of negative thoughts, and to learn to avoid them or stop them before they get out of hand. Almost anything can be a trigger to a negative emotion, but it's the way you react to a trigger that decides whether it turns into a negative thought or behavior, or whether you simply register it and let it go.

Get into the habit of analyzing your anger. Is there a pattern? Is it getting worse? How often does it happen? Are triggers always the same? If you know where your anger is coming from, you can either avoid the triggers or be mentally prepared to face them.

It's the way you interpret a thought, a memory, a comment someone makes, or an event that either improves or clouds your judgment. This is why negative self-talk can be so destructive.

3. Cultivate a nurturing environment

People in your environment can be a pillar of comfort and support or a cause of constant sabotage. They can help pick you up when you're down, or make you feel even worse about yourself than you already do. This is why choosing your company is so important, especially if you are oversensitive and tend to take things personally, or have a problem controlling your temper. If your reaction is easily triggered, and especially if you have a history of violence, you should try to surround yourself with people who are least likely to push your buttons.

This is not always possible, but what is possible is for you to make some changes in your behavior or daily routine to better avoid situations which make you angry. For example, if you have a problem with road rage, consider taking public transport or finding an alternative route to work. If you have a problem with certain individuals, try to get them to meet you on neutral ground, like in a coffee shop or a park, rather than at their office or home, where being on their "territory" may make you feel more vulnerable and less in control of your emotions.

4. Respond quickly to negative emotions

How quickly you react to a negative thought will decide how successful you are in preventing that thought from becoming a thought pattern. Negativity breeds negativity, so the trick is to prevent a negative thought from becoming a negative emotion, which can become a negative reaction.

5. Learn to identify your threshold

Sometimes, a change of scene is all it takes for anger to subside. This could mean walking away from your office for a few moments, from your flat for a couple of hours, or moving away from your parents' home. Many conflicts happen as a result of a lack of "breathing space," so when you feel you're beginning to get angry, if possible, remove yourself from that environment for a while.

Some people can quickly come up with ideas about how to respond to an anger trigger, others need more time to think about how to react. Although it's not possible to walk away in the middle of an important meeting or a job interview, when you feel anger rising, at least take a couple of moments to compose yourself. Simply, count to ten or take a few deep breaths before responding.

6. **Weaken your triggers if you can't prevent them**

Learn how to think rationally so you can calm yourself down when under stress and don't take it out on others. A negative thought allowed to get out of hand can lead to rage which is often targeted at those who happen to be around, even if they have nothing to do with your problem.

If avoiding a trigger fails to work, at least try to weaken it by developing a positive thought or repeating a positive affirmation which will counter the negative thought that makes you angry—if you think you are not popular, think of those who actually enjoy spending time with you; if you're angry with yourself for being overweight, think of all those people who were once overweight, and managed to get fit through their own efforts.

If you feel very negative and nothing seems to make it better, try doing something drastic. First of all, leave the place where the negative thought happened, and avoid reading or watching any negative material (like news dealing with war, terrorism, or the destructive effects of climate change). Don't talk to those who are always complaining, sad, or depressed. Although watching news can serve as a distraction from your negative thoughts, it can also make them worse. Fear-provoking news, movies, or sermons will only feed your negativity, while what you need to do is starve it of energy.

7. Improve communication skills

Lack of communication is very often the main cause of misunderstandings, arguments, or angry scenes. When you learn to communicate effectively and know how to express your feelings, you will see that many of the situations which make you angry will disappear. Most people prefer talking to listening and, very often, this is where the problem lies. For example, if you had listened carefully, you would have understood what the client really wanted, or if you let your friends know how much it upsets you when they mention your acne problem, you wouldn't end up angry and hurt every time someone brings this up.

8. Challenge your thinking

It's not easy to admit you were wrong. After you have identified your anger triggers, ask yourself if perhaps there may be other reasons for your anger which the triggers have masked? What if what you think someone meant is not true? Is there another way to think about the incident that provoked such a violent reaction in you? Challenging yourself takes courage and maturity, but you'll be surprised what you can find if you dig deep enough.

A negative mindset is never the result of a single negative thought. It is the consequence of a series of negative thoughts which you have lived with for some time—maybe all your life. Be mindful of your environment, the people you socialize with, and the things you read and watch, as all that contributes to your state of mind.

Day 20

Nutrition for Stress Relief

Your diet is not only the fuel that keeps you going, it also affects how often you'll get sick, how quickly you'll recover, how much weight you'll gain, how long you'll live, and more.

There is a reason Hippocrates said, "Let thy food be thy medicine and thy medicine be thy food."

Diet does not only help maintain good health, it can also be used as a natural medicine to correct certain imbalances—more fiber will improve digestion, less unhealthy fats will reduce your chances of heart disease, less salt will lower your blood pressure, antioxidant-rich foods will lower your risk of cancer.

Mood-enhancing plants can be used to soothe a troubled mind and ease many psychological problems, and you don't have to be ill to reap these benefits. You can use them to lift your spirits, bring tranquility, calm down, achieve mental clarity, or aid meditation.

According to Ayurveda, combining foods of different colors is the best way to eat, but a new study reveals that this kind of diet is not only nutritious and physically healthy, but is also good for your mood—different colors carry different energies and these have a direct influence on your mood. Whether you are aware of it or not, color stimulates your emotions and motivates your decisions.

Fight Mental Disorders with Nutrition

Although we are all affected by stress, not everyone knows that it can be controlled with a diet. Certain foods provide natural protection from stress simply because they increase the levels of hormones in the body that naturally fight stress. As well, there are foods and beverages that reduce stress by lowering the levels of hormones that trigger them.

7 foods that help you beat stress:

1. **A warm drink**

   We all know that a cup of tea will calm you down, a cup of warm milk or cocoa before going to bed will help you sleep peacefully, and that a cup of soup helps if you're not feeling well. It's not so much the nutrients from these drinks that provide a sense of calm and healing, but the warmth of the beverage itself. For a number of reasons, there's something very comforting about a warm drink.

2. **Dark chocolate**

   As all chocolate lovers know, the taste and smell of chocolate alone are enough to reduce stress. Besides, dark chocolate is rich in antioxidants, which are known to fight stress as well as protect the body from free radicals. If taken daily, it can help you improve your heart health, lower the blood pressure, prevent some types of cancer, as well as produce endorphins which will improve your mood. If taking it daily, you shouldn't take more than 30 grams.

3. **Healthy Carbs**

Carbohydrates increase levels of serotonin, a chemical that boosts mood and reduces stress, which indirectly improves cognitive function. However, there are healthy and unhealthy carbs. To improve your mood and reduce stress-induced anger, include the following foods in your daily diet: sweet potato, brown rice, oats, quinoa, buckwheat, beetroots, beans, chickpeas, carrots, mangos, bananas, blueberries, and apples.

4. **Avocados**

Rich in omega-3 fatty acids, this is one of the healthiest fruits you can eat. These essential acids are known to reduce stress and anxiety, boost concentration, and improve mood.

5. **Fatty fish**

Another great source of omega-3 fatty acids, which not only beat stress but ease depression. The best source of omega-3 fatty acids are tuna, halibut, salmon, herring, mackerel, sardines, and lake trout.

6. **Nuts**

Nuts are full of vitamins and healthy fatty acids. They are particularly rich in vitamin B which neutralizes the effects of stress. Add almonds, pistachios, or walnuts to fruit or vegetable salads, muesli, yogurt, or soups.

7. **Vitamin C**

High levels of vitamin C help reduce stress, so eat fresh fruit and vegetables or take supplements.

Our bodies respond to threatening situations by sending signals to the brain that it's in trouble. The brain reacts by requiring food that will help it think more clearly and be ready for a physical response—fight or flight.

The main threat we face today is that of prolonged stress, which our bodies react to in the same way as when confronted with physical danger. However, after the threat has passed or after you've escaped, your body goes into a recovery mode characterized by an increased appetite to recover from the shock and exhaustion. It is at this stage that many people reach for comfort foods to calm down and recover the energy lost during a stressful situation.

This is how most of us fight stress. However, there is a healthier approach to stress-relief.

3 tips on how to manage stress with diet:

- On a stressful day, eat less and more often.
- Eat plenty of fruits and vegetables to get the nutrients needed for fighting stress.

- Avoid or limit caffeine-rich foods, such as coffee, tea, soft drinks, and chocolate.

Nutrition and Anger Management

Anger behavior ranges from screaming into a pillow or going for a run all, all the way up to murder, and as many people with anger problems end up in jail, even mild anger outbursts should not be ignored—especially if they happen repeatedly. There are different ways of treating anger disorders, one of the easiest being with a healthy diet.

Studies suggest that uncontrollable outbursts of anger are only one of the many symptoms of various mood disorders, like depression, anxiety, insomnia, addiction, and so on. Interestingly, most such individuals have hypoglycemia—a sugar handling problem.

The reason hypoglycemia is common in chronically angry individuals is because such people are often exposed to unnaturally high levels of adrenaline. In stressful situations, when the brain anticipates energy starvation, it triggers the secretion of adrenaline.

When that happens, there is a rush of adrenaline to feed the brain, as well as activation of the fight/flight hormone. In such a state, people become either defensive or aggressive.

Fortunately, this problem can be solved without drugs through a hypoglycemic diet based on four simple rules:

1. Avoid sugar and sugar-rich foods

2. Eat high-protein foods (fish, eggs, chicken, beef)

3. Snack every three hours on complex carbohydrate foods, including whole grains, fruits, legumes, green vegetables, and starchy vegetables, to help with the slow release of glucose

4. Eat plenty of green vegetables and fresh fruits

5. Take supplements such as vitamin B-complex, vitamin C, vitamin D, and probiotics.

Those who follow a hypoglycemic diet quickly normalize their blood sugar levels and stress hormones adrenaline and cortisol, which are responsible for mood swings, depression, anxiety, alcoholism, and other mental disorders that often lead to angry outbursts.

More and more scientists believe that what we eat contributes to how angry we feel, and numerous studies show that a diet high in trans fatty acids is directly linked to increased aggression.

Trans fats are unhealthy fats found in the foods we enjoy the most—French fries, fried and battered foods, pies, margarine sticks, shortening, frostings, pancakes and waffles, ice cream, ground beef, processed meats, cookies and cakes, biscuits, crackers, frozen dinners, and canned chili.

Giving up your favorite foods is not easy and is best done gradually over a couple of months, otherwise you may not be able to cope with the cravings. However, if you're struggling with an anger problem and know that nutrient deficiency is a major cause of your behavioral abnormalities, switching to a healthy eating plan will make a significant improvement.

The reason processed foods are so bad for your health is that they are nothing more than empty calories, which not only lack nutrition but also contain a lot of unhealthy color and taste additives. Only with a healthy diet will your body be able to produce the chemicals and hormones it needs for clear thinking, healthy mood, and balanced emotions.

In conclusion, you can keep your anger problem under control without therapy if you change your diet and stick to it.

Try a mood-stabilizing diet for a month, and see how your behavior changes and your mood improves. As Bethenny Frankel pointed out, "Your diet is a bank account. Good food choices are a good investment."

Mood-stabilizing diet:

1. Mood-boosting foods: fruits and vegetables—the less processed, the better

2. Plenty of dopamine-building foods: fish, poultry, eggs, and leafy greens

3. Omega-3 rich foods to fight depression: fish, flaxseed, chia seeds, walnuts

4. Magnesium-rich foods to support sleep and relaxation: almonds, spinach, pumpkin seeds, sunflower seeds

5. Vitamin D-rich foods to prevent mood disorders: fatty fish, egg yolks, liver

6. Limit sugar

Day 21

Putting It All Together

The idea behind writing this book was to showcase how you can transform your life by taking control of your thoughts. And when you control your thoughts, you can better control your emotions and your behavior.

In the stressful time we live in, our patience and tolerance are often challenged. Stress typically leads to more stress, and mental health problems are often the result of this vicious circle.

Negativity is a common side effect of chronic stress, as is poor anger management. And the reason people develop a negative mindset is often not because they have a negative attitude to life, but because they are overwhelmed by stress and anxiety.

So, how do you break this circle of stress-negativity-more stress-anger-more stress-more-negativity? By understanding where all this negativity is coming from, and by acknowledging that many times it is not stress, but your own self-limiting thoughts that make you see everything in a negative light.

Unfortunately, becoming positive doesn't happen overnight, nor can it happen on its own. That's something that has to be worked on, and that usually includes making some big, life-changing decisions.

Remap Your Mind

In a culture obsessed with youth, beauty, and fitness, one is constantly reminded of what they should look like. As a result, we have a trillion-dollar health and wellness industry which cashes in on the idea that there is no reason we should not all have perfect bodies, beautiful white teeth, and flawless skin.

However, while taking care of your body is important for your well-being, it doesn't mean you should neglect the part that often stays well-hidden, sometimes even from you—your mind. And just because your emotions and thoughts cannot be seen, while your teeth, body, and hair can, doesn't mean they are any less important.

In the overpopulated, fast, and competitive world of ours, it's easy to reach a stage where you become so overwhelmed with life that you can no longer keep track of all the changes taking place around you. Your brain can only take so much—when it can no longer manage the overload, it may respond by developing a mental health disorder.

If you can't manage your thoughts and feelings, you start living on auto-pilot: barely keeping your head above water, struggling to deal with the stress, fear, and anger that your life seems to be full of. Is it surprising that mental disorders are spreading like wildfire? Some studies even suggest that poverty is not the main reason for the rise in recorded crime, but the real reason is the increasing number of stressors that people are just not coping with.

So, when you hit a low point in life—or even better, before you do—why not do something to prevent the emotions of anger, frustration, and sadness from taking over your life? Take responsibility for what you are going through, but don't give in to defeat.

If you can afford it, go on a mental makeover retreat. If you can't, you can turn over a new leaf by giving yourself a mental makeover without leaving the comfort of your home. Just like you can revamp your body, you can remap your mind with a new approach to life.

Mental Makeover

Mental makeover techniques are about successfully overcoming challenges, taking control of your emotions, and staying healthy and happy. They revolve around high self-esteem and a positive attitude.

10 tips on mental makeover:

1. **Know yourself**

   When you know yourself, you understand what situations make you feel uncomfortable and you avoid them when you can, or you come up with ways to deal with them in an emotionally-intelligent way. There is no recipe for happiness and contentment—it's good to understand what makes you happy so you can do more of it.

2. Take control of your emotions

For good mental health, it's very important not to hold grudges or keep emotions bottled up. While the best way to let go of unexpressed emotions is to talk about them, if there are issues you don't feel like discussing or if you have no one to talk to, you can choose a non-verbal way of communication—writing, journaling, painting, singing, or dancing. The trick is to learn to express your emotions in a way that's not offensive to others or harmful to you.

3. Keep your brain in shape

The reason the mind deteriorates so quickly once people go into retirement is that it's no longer stimulated. While you work, you are constantly under some kind of stress and pressure, and although this can be bad for your health, it keeps your mind alert.

To prevent, or at least slow, mental deterioration, think of games or activities that would keep your brain occupied. If you lack company, get a pet. If you like reading, join a library. Go for lectures, do crosswords, play sports, join a club, learn a new language or skill. When you cultivate new interests, you open the door to new people and new experiences in your life.

4. Learn to enjoy life

Why is this so hard? Some people feel uncomfortable, even guilty when they're enjoying themselves. Others don't know how to do it. Some feel it's a luxury they can't afford. Enjoying life is about finding pleasure in what you do, and it's not a luxury for it does not have to cost you anything.

Depending on your financial situation, it could be something as extravagant as an exotic vacation or as simple as meeting a friend for coffee, planting some flowers in your garden, or taking part in a dog show. Learning to enjoy life is about finding a way to feel happy, regardless of what you do or where you are. Enjoying life is about being happy to be alive.

5. Meditate

Meditation is a great way to still your mind and stop the inner chatter so you can "hear" the important stuff. Long-term daily meditation improves your health, and actually rewires your brain so you become calmer and better able to handle difficult situations. You also become more open-hearted and able to see things from others' points of view. In other words, you become more emotionally intelligent. It may sound like a cliché, but meditation does change people.

6. Cultivate mindfulness

If you embrace mindfulness as a way of life, you choose to be fully aware of your thoughts and emotions. The reason mindfulness is so important for your mental health is that it makes you feel "centered" and helps you cope with whatever life throws at you. It also improves your physical health by relieving stress, and can even reduce chronic pain. When you live mindfully, you are fully present in whatever situation you may find yourself.

7. Focus on what you want, not on what you don't want

One of the best ways to develop a positive mindset is to shift your mind from what you DON'T WANT and DON'T HAVE, and from what you CAN'T DO, to what you do want, have, and know. However, you have to approach this mindfully, because focus without intention gets you what you don't want.

8. Healthy diet

Food has a very real effect on our physical performance (by providing energy), mental activity (by providing mental clarity through vitamin- and antioxidant-rich foods), and emotions (by calming or alerting us, like chocolate, sugar, caffeine, tea). For long-term wellness, choose a diet that supports you on all levels of your being.

9. Boost your self-image

A true mental makeover is impossible if you struggle with low self-esteem. This is about how you think about yourself, what your appearance says about you, and how approachable you are. Without a positive self-image, you'll find it hard to get far in life. Perhaps the easiest way to improve your self-image is to think about yourself as you would like to be. As Napoleon Hill pointed out, "What the mind can conceive and believe, it can achieve."

10.   Develop emotional intelligence

If your life is not too unbalanced, most of your mental blocks can be overcome by developing emotional intelligence skills, which you can learn from self-help books such as this one or from attending an emotional intelligence course. As an emotionally intelligent person, you will always be in touch with your inner world and rely on your self-awareness to guide you when making a decision.

Perhaps, the success of mental makeover depends on how much you believe in yourself. As Roy Bennett put it, "You are braver than you think, more talented than you know, and capable of more than you imagine."

Thank you

Before you go, I just wanted to say thank you for purchasing my book.

You could have picked from dozens of other books on the same topic, but you chose this one.

So, a HUGE thanks to you for getting this book and for reading all the way to the end.

Now, I wanted to ask you for a small favor. **Could you please consider posting a review on the platform? Reviews are one of the easiest ways to support the work of authors.**

This feedback will help me continue to write the type of books that will help you get the results you want. So, if you enjoyed it, please let me know.

Lastly, don't forget to grab a copy of your Free Bonus book *"Bulletproof Confidence Checklist."* If you want to learn how to overcome shyness and social anxiety and become more confident, then this book is for you.
Just go to:

https://theartofmastery.com/confidence/